16

NO CAUSE FOR PANIC

By the Same Author:

AN AMERICAN IN WASHINGTON

No Cause For Panic

By RUSSELL BAKER

J. B. LIPPINCOTT COMPANY

Philadelphia and New York

First Edition

Printed in the United States of America

Library of Congress Catalog Card Number: 64–7507

CONTENTS

PART 1

THE AMERICAN WAY OF LIFE

NGUYEN NGOC WHO?

Something really has to be done about this crisis glut. It is getting as bad as the farm surplus.

At one point recently crisis connoisseurs counted twelve crises running simultaneously—in Borneo, the Congo, Cyprus, East Germany, France, Kenya, Laos, Panama, Tanganyika, Uganda, Vietnam and Zanzibar.

It is too much. The State Department may have resources to cope with twelve crises a week, but the rest of us haven't. The average person cannot worry efficiently about more than one crisis every fifteen days, as analysis of any typical daily worry schedule will illustrate.

The typical citizen rises in the morning to a confrontation with the mirror, which starts him worrying about his own mortality. At breakfast, his schedule demands twenty minutes of worry about the children's table manners and the decay of their wardrobes, which inexorably leads him to worry about the decay of his own wardrobe, his house and his car.

This brings him to the brink of worry about money, but this is deferred for the after-dinner worry slot. Wisdom has it that men who worry about money while their wives are still in hair curlers are frequently divorced. Breakfast does, however, allow perhaps twenty minutes with the newspapers.

The typical reader divides the time among the comics (worry: is Tracy gaining weight?); the sports section (worry: will Charles Finley break up the American League? and why shouldn't he?); and the news (worry, worry, worry: can the Republicans ever make a comeback? Shouldn't Lyndon Johnson slow down? Where is Zanzibar, who is John Okello and why in the world is he flying to Pemba? And what is Pemba, anyhow?).

At the most, there are seven minutes for weighing crises before heading for work, and the trip to work is again absorbed in worries about mortality. Is the smoking report really true? Can his 40-a-day habit be broken? What about all those martinis? Shouldn't he see his doctor, eat less fried food, have an electrocardiogram, a chest X-ray, get more exercise, have his glasses changed, get a haircut, have his shoes resoled, get the car greased, remember his wife's birthday, telephone his grandmother, read more?

The day is taken up with occupational worries. Where shall he eat lunch? How to make the rest of the office sweat in the morning conference? Are two martinis too much at lunch? Has that stenographer started drinking at lunch too? Who runs the office, anyhow, after lunch?

Evenings are for worrying about his family—the children's school problems, the household bills, the water seeping through the living room ceiling. Are the children beginning to laugh at him when his back is turned? Are the neighbors sneering because his car is getting old?

Finally, there are seventeen minutes for worrying about the state of the world. It is a mess. Back in the old days, there was one crisis which went on for years. Diplomats were constantly getting together in Paris or Moscow or London and parleying, and their parleys were always collapsing. This was known as the cold war. It was very easy to understand. Us versus Them. White hats against the black hats.

Now, instead of Us and Them, the papers are full of phenomena like Nguyen Ngoc Tho, Hai Huu Xuan, Souvanouvong and Okello. Who is Okello? Why has he flown to Pemba? Where is Pemba?

It requires great application to grasp all this, and the question that intrudes on the lesson is: Is this crisis really worth understanding? How often have we struggled to master a preposterous crisis situation—the 1962 Haitian crisis comes immediately to mind—only to discover that by the time we understand it, nobody else cares. Most crises nowadays are over before you can say Neo Lao Hak Xat.

What we need is a crisis meter. It should register the intensity of crises on an ascending scale from one to ten. A reading of ten would indicate a crisis which, in the long run, might be as important to the man in the street as the World Series. Everybody would willingly bone up on a real number ten crisis, and leave the rest to the pros.

Then we wouldn't have to sit around worrying because we haven't worried enough about Okello to find out who he is.

"INCREDIBLE, SHEM!"

"Meet the fabulous Noodles, ladies and gentlemen, fresh from the cheers of the crowned heads. First of all, here is young Kiddo Noodle, founder of the group and its spokesman. What is it that you don't do, Kiddo?"

"I'm the one who doesn't sing, Jack."

"Didn't you sing at one time though, Kiddo?"

"Oh yes, I used to sing quite a bit and made several fine records, but there was no future in it. Then I got the idea of becoming a nonsinger and my records really started to take off."

"Marvelous, Kiddo. Do you think your distinctive costume had anything to do with your success?"

"Well, Jack, you see, when you get out there on the stage with that guitar and you start to not sing, I think you can just drive those little girls crazy without wearing black leather jeans and having all that chest hair hanging out of your shirt, see? I mean, those little girls are so wild to have a little mediocrity they can call their own that they'd scream for me in a double-breasted suit and a clean jaw."

"Fantastic, Kiddo. Now why don't you introduce us all to the other three Noodles?"

"Gladly, Jack; first off, here is the one and only Leda."

"This is indeed an honor, Leda. I suppose you are the world's most publicized bad actress."

"Yes, I am certainly the worst of the best-known actresses—"

"—and the highest paid of course. How did you become such a poor actress, Leda?"

"I owe it all to my mother, Jack. She saw quite early that the real future in this country lay in cultivating a non-talent. 'This country,' she told me, 'is full of singers who can't sing, painters who can't paint and actors who can't act—and they're all making a million dollars.' I started the struggle for mediocrity when I was still a baby."

"Amazing, Leda. But of course, having the most beautiful calves in films don't hurt any, either. Now, folks, our third Noodle is Shem the Bearded, whose canvases hang in the duplexes of the most sophisticated suckers of two continents. Congratulations, Shem, on those really ridiculous paintings."

"Thank you, Jack, but in all candor I must confess that I started out trying to paint good pictures, and I'd still be starving today if Kiddo here hadn't been looking for a painter to join the Noodles. Kiddo put me onto the beard and the Raymond Duncan toga and Leda suggested I call my work 'transverse dynamism.' "

"Incredible, Shem! Transverse dynamism really swept the art world, after that first performance on Ed Sullivan."

"Yes, and it was quite by accident, too. This chimp from an animal act broke loose and tracked through my paints and then started climbing the wall. Do you know that wall sold for $90,000?"

"Magnificent, Shem! Really forgetable work you're doing! And now, finally, here is Apollo Noodle. You all know him, ladies and gentlemen. Give him a big hand. Apollo, tell the audience about your non-talent."

"Gladly, Jack. I guest."

"Would you explain, Apollo?"

"Well, you see, Jack, this country is full of television shows and there isn't enough material to keep them all running. To pad out the time, they need guests—people who can't sing, or act, or paint, or do anything. I'm a guest. I come on camera and I let all my inner dullness seep out into the show. The people watching at home feel flattered by the discovery that there is somebody more boring than they are, and they love the show."

SOMETIMES PEANUTS ARE UNWELCOME

Roy Gallant, writing in the magazine *Nature and Science,* urges people to quit smiling at chimpanzees. This is sensible advice. People who begin by smiling at chimpanzees sometimes wind up talking to bears.

Mr. Gallant's advice is based on studies conducted by Dr. Desmond Morris, curator of mammals at the London Zoo. When a chimpanzee sees two rows of human teeth, he is not amused, according to Dr. Morris, but angered and frightened, and bares his own teeth in return.

The person smiling at the chimp misinterprets the ape's response, assumes that the chimp is smiling back at him, and smiles harder, thus infuriating the chimp and starting him down the road to neurosis.

It is not surprising that the chimpanzee resents being smiled at all the time. One need only put one self in the chimp's shoes to appreciate his resentment. It is no picnic sitting behind bars having peanuts thrown at you by smilers.

This raises some unpleasant questions about the whole smile tradition in this country from zoo to White House. The theory behind it has always been that if you smile, the world will smile with you. Politicians, who are the most indefatigable smilers, hold that a handsome set of incisors is more valuable than a brain for winning elections, and even the solemn professions like undertaking and nuclear science assume that the smile is sound business practice.

The papers are full of smilers. A general tells Congress that the world's nuclear storehouse is now big enough to provide the equivalent of a 35-ton dynamite explosion for each individual on earth, and the illustrating picture shows him smiling.

Barry Goldwater declares that the country is going to ruin, and smiles and smiles. At less cosmic levels, everybody can recite ugly experiences associated with smiles. There is the smile of the dentist when he says, "This may hurt a little—" The smile of the banker declaring you a hopeless credit risk. And the smile of the TV repairman explaining that he will have to take the set back to the shop.

If incoming smiles too often mean misery, outgoing smiles are likely to mean trouble. Smile while walking through any public square in America, and the panhandlers attack in platoons. What man has not let his smile at some time or other come to rest on a lovely stranger across a crowded room, only to note her escort glaring back with undisguised malevolence?

The British ration their smiles. When they use one, it is effective. No one has ever seen a picture of a British politician smiling, although they are always announcing that Britain is going to ruin. Of course, the British do have that odd habit of smiling at dogs, but this is probably sounder than the American habit of smiling back at politicians.

The French think that the smile is overdone in America and favor less ambiguous gestures. A Frenchman, for example, will not smile at your wife across a crowded room; he will walk across, dismiss you and ask her what she is doing tomorrow afternoon. French politicians also know better than to smile at the voters. One could no more picture President de Gaulle smiling than imagine a toastmaster calling him "Chuck."

Precisely when or why Americans adopted the smile as the national facial expression is unclear. There are no portraits of George Washington, Jefferson or Jackson smiling, and the one photograph of a Lincoln smile is a tragedy. Yet nowadays the whole country, in Scott Fitzgerald's phrase, lives by the contorted pan.

The trouble is not so much that it is ridiculous to get elected on strong teeth, or look cheerful about "overkill," or act happy about charging some wretch $67.50 for TV repairs. The trouble is that the smile becomes debased in the process.

People who are constantly smiled at by generals who have 35 tons of dynamite earmarked for them or by TV repairmen planning to deplete their bank balance are apt to reconsider the value of the smile and agree with Shakespeare that "one may smile, and smile, and be a villain."

In extreme cases, these people may develop hallucinations about being behind bars with peanuts raining in on them. Sometimes they go mad with the urge to bite back when they see two exposed rows of human teeth.

STYX ON SMUT

The expulsion of the so-called Sanitized Seven from the Society of Suitable Writers and their subsequent announcement that they will start legal proceedings for reinstatement have left the cultural community divided and embittered.

While there is no respectable support for the kind of book or play that the Seven have been publishing clandestinely in Paris, many eminent authors nevertheless feel that they should not be censured until the courts have ruled on the basic issue, which is, of course, clean books.

The vehicle which the Seven will use to get their case into court is the infamous "Love on Credit," which a generation of Americans has bought at $7.50 a copy from Seine bookstalls and brought home to hide under the mattress. Not even its author, the dollar-canny Sam Jim, whose books have earned a fortune in under-the-counter sales, has ever claimed literary merit for "Love on Credit."

"Quite frankly," Jim admitted the other day, "I wrote it, pure and simple, as a clean book. I wanted to cash in on the public's secret desire to read something a little less racy than you can get at the drugstore."

The plot can only be sketchily suggested. Suffice it to say that "Love on Credit" is a story about a male and a female (both human beings) who fall in love with each other, marry (each other!) and live happily on charge accounts.

Ten years ago one American publishing house, impressed by the book's Paris sales, approached Sam Jim for permission to publish a dirtied-up version suitable for the American market. The plan was to redraw the male character as a drug addict, do away with the marriage and rewrite the female character as an Oriental midget with an infantile attachment to a sinister orangutan.

"I laughed in their faces," Jim said. "If that book had ever been published under my title, it would have ruined my following. My fans would have said, 'Jim's beginning to compromise now that he's struck it rich. He's going respectable.' "

Jim and his six expelled colleagues plan to make a public sale of "Love on Credit" and invite arrest on charges of violating the literary code. There is no hard and fast legal definition, of course, of what constitutes a clean book; and the Seven believe they have a good chance of winning a court test.

Rob Nightshade, whose notorious "Jolly Twins" trilogy is the hottest item in the nation's fraternity houses this semester, describes the Seven's thinking in these words: "We know that vast segments of America may not be ready for clean books, but we contend that the minority which is tired of literary rape and horsewhipping should be entitled to books showing life as it really is."

The man who forced expulsion of the Seven was Thor Styx, author of "Vile Alleys" and its stage adaptation, "A Bed Full of Moss." "Life is a filthy business," he said, in explaining his detestation of clean books. "The only thing that makes it tolerable is a good dirty book.

"Take the typical American. After a typical working day, he takes the bus or subway home feeling life is hardly worth living. Then he starts reading one of my novels with a really sick, squalid view of life. By the time he gets home, his own life seems fairly decent by comparison. If his wife is depressed, he can take her to see one of my dirty plays or movies, and their own lives no longer seem so awful."

Styx asserts that clean books, on the other hand, pander to the basest human appetite for escape. When the reader puts one down, Styx says, he finds the real world, by contrast, sordid and depressing.

Cynics say that Styx's real motives may be more selfish than all this implies. If clean books were to make a comeback, they say, Styx would be caught with an unmarketable glut of four-letter ideas.

THE STEAK WORSHIPERS

The American affair with beefsteak has entered a new phase. Its manifestation is the great steak-house epidemic now raging across the country.

Stop in a strange town and ask the natives to suggest a good restaurant and they will invariably direct you to a place called the Flame, the Fiery Pit or the Burning Six-Shooter. Whatever the name, it will turn out to be a steak house. It is clear that while the social historians were busy sneering about a nation enthralled by the back-yard barbecue pit, the country has been moving out of the back yard and into the steak house.

The new steak houses are not to be confused with the old steak-and-chop houses. Steak-and-chop houses had sawdust on the floor and a long black bar with Texas Longhorns mounted over the mirror and faded glossy prints on the wall autographed by old vaudeville headliners and 1915 ball-players who had gotten soused in the back booth.

The new steak houses are distantly related to the steak-and-chop houses, as the 1964 Cadillac is related to the Locomobile, but spiritually the two are light-years apart. For one thing, there are the constantly blazing fires. In the chop house, the fire was kept back in the kitchen, which the guests were always invited to inspect but which no guest in his right mind ever set foot in.

The steak house brings the fire out of the kitchen and puts it right among the diners. Sometimes girls in cowgirl suits and black fish-net hose rush among the tables carrying fire with them. The headwaiter frequently punishes the scrubbier-looking guests by seating them against the great fire jets where their eyebrows get singed.

The reasons for all this public fire are obscure, but the steak-house owners consider it indispensable to success. As the operator of a Chicago watering place famed for its fire rites once explained, "The customers seem to like it and it don't hurt the food none."

All the best steak houses costume their help in what they conceive to be cowpunching garb. Waiters in hairy chaps and bandannas are not uncommon. The better steak houses use kerosene lamps fitted with ingenious electric bulbs that throw a ghastly flickering light.

The result is something eerily suggestive of a temple built to satisfy a nation of steak cultists. The behavior of the worshipers is as ritualistically fixed as the decor of fire, servers' garb and Old West relics.

Upon entering a steak house, for example, the guest immediately orders a martini. It is always warm, and the guest knows that it will always be warm. With all that fire it has to be. And yet he orders a martini because a martini is what people who go to steak houses order. To order a sazerac would invite public humiliation.

He orders a steak. He orders it rare. He may order it medium-rare if he does not mind being sneered at by waiters in hairy chaps, but if he orders it well done the manager may come and tell him that he has poor taste.

He orders a green salad with Roquefort cheese. Roquefort cheese invariably costs 25 cents extra, and usually it is not Roquefort cheese at all but a domestic blue cheese. Nevertheless, he orders Roquefort cheese and pays the 25 cents because that is part of the rite, like the fire and the warm martini and the rare steak.

The social historians have no explanation for the triumph of the steak house. And yet, all over the country, the steak houses are bursting forth in flames, and restaurants that once specialized in spaghetti, escargots, lobster and couscous are rapidly converting to steak.

In the absence of documentation, we can only theorize about the reasons. Could it be that old dad, who spent the last decade drinking warm martinis while slaving over the back-yard grill, has finally revolted and decided to transfer the rite to an institutional setting? Could it be that steak worship is beginning to dominate American society?

Or could it be that all those years of back-yard cooking have finally destroyed American gastronomy? It was always a frail child.

DE GAULLE'S AMERICA

The most satisfying way ever devised for settling old scores among nations is the tourist guidebook. When artfully written, it incorporates the elegant sneer and the gratuitous insult under the smile of brotherhood. For nearly twenty years, the guidebook attack has been almost entirely an American resource, but now that Europeans are beginning to come here for vacations the Americans are getting a taste of their own medicine. Here, translated from a popular French guide to America, entitled "The Manischewitz Drinkers," is an illustration of just what can be done without firing a shot.

"So you are making the voyage to America! How amusing

you will find these proud members of the Anglo-Saxon family, whose very existence is owed to the French foreign policy of the eighteenth century. Noted for their massive Philistinism and cultural deprivation, the Americans are nonetheless a warm and friendly people who amuse themselves in such charming pastimes as the baseball, the movies with happy endings and the dog racing at such tiresome spas as Miami Beach.

"Tourists in America this year will enjoy also the enchanting spectacle of the Presidential election campaign. The Frenchman, inured no doubt to the sobriety of European politics, will find himself always delighted by the refreshing techniques of the so-called front-runners and dark horses, as they fly about the nation eating chicken dinners and dispensing what the natives call 'bologna.'

"These front-runners and dark horses, naturally, are seeking the office of President, which is at present occupied by the Grand Texan, Lyndon Johnson. President de Gaulle so esteems the Grand Texan that he has offered to grant him an audience, and therefore one will not be surprised to hear that the Grand Texan is considered invincible in the forthcoming election.

"Fortunately for the tourist, M. Johnson's invincibility does not discourage various millionaires—men who have no doubt tired of business and the obscurity of their clubs—from arraying themselves as front-runners and dark horses and flying all over dispensing the bologna.

"The tourist may well encounter one of these chic millionaires on some street corner in the provinces, or even while dining at one of the nation's many execrable lunch counters, for they roll gaily through the streets and mercantile places accosting pedestrian and shopper alike.

"Who are some of the more imposing front-runners? There is the charming Goldwater, whose philosophy would have sent him gallantly to the guillotine in 1793. There is the gregarious Rockefeller, more widely known in France perhaps as 'Le Duc D'Essence.' No Frenchman should come home without having seen this prodigious front-runner consume one of his country's abominable hot dogs on a street corner.

"One will naturally desire also to have some personal contact with the Grand Texan, who, being invincible, will not be readily available at provincial street corners. Such an opportunity may well present itself if you have the good fortune to be the house guest of some amiable resident of Washington.

"The tourist will be amused from time to time to hear the various campaigners discuss the election as though President de Gaulle did not exist. They will, for example, refer to the American Presidency as 'the most powerful office on earth' and assert that 'the leadership of the free world is at stake.'

"It would be inexcusable for the guest from abroad to observe to them that no matter who may emerge the victor in America, President de Gaulle will go on.

"*Alors,* to dispose of a few political questions; how long does this gay Presidential campaigning continue? It will proceed excessively until November, when it will pause. A new season will open in early 1965 and run continuously for four years.

"Can one obtain a book that will explain how successful government is possible in a state of perpetual Presidential campaigning? No.

"What should one do upon encountering a dark horse who insists upon buying one an abominable hot dog? One should say, 'M. Dark Horse, I would not eat a hot dog on this street corner even with General de Gaulle.' "

DEAR BORIS KARLOFF

Everybody knows that this country has a critical shortage of heroes suitable for small boys, but nobody seems to be worrying about it.

There are various reasons for the shortage. One is the national propensity for rapid consumption. We are not only the world's most conspicuous consumers of everything from plastic telephone dialers to celluloid gunslingers, but also the world's fastest. Nowadays we use up a new car style in two years and a crooner in ten months.

We consume our heroes even faster, probably because they are so few. John Glenn and Alan Shepard were not only household names before the headline ink had dried on their exploits; they were household guests for weeks afterwards, thanks to the nation's astounding communications machinery which now tells you ten times more than you want to know about everything, including heroes.

As a result, when Scott Carpenter flew the country's second earth orbit, the feat seemed almost routine until it appeared that Carpenter had been lost at sea. And when Walter Schirra flew the third, some people were annoyed because the television coverage interfered with coverage of a Dodgers-Giants baseball game in California.

In addition, American business nowadays seems incapable of seeing a hero without trying to turn him into a salesman. Men like Frank Gifford and Paul Hornung, who might qualify as frontline football heroes, were for years turning up on TV or radio pushing cigarettes.

A generation ago, the athletic heroes might have pushed Wheaties, arguing that cereal in the morning improved the muscle tone, but the athlete who smoked and let the news get around lost status in the short-pants set all over the country.

Basically, of course, this is an anti-hero society, except in politics. This may be because of the triumph of the organization, which cherishes the cog and the cypher. In a society of cogs and cyphers and square pegs in square holes, stability depends upon keeping the parts persuaded that there is heroism in being unheroic.

And so, we get absurdities like the radio promotion being used in Washington by D.C. Transit, the local bus company. In this, an announcer declares that "one of the foremost missions" of the D.C. Transit driver is to get us to our "destination" safely and on time. With this treatment, the routine bus driver's job of getting the bureaucrats downtown in the rush hour becomes a heroic "mission" in a class with taking a B-17 into the flak at Schweinfurt.

In any case, authentic heroes are now so scarce that this country may have an incipient socio-psychological problem on its hands. This is the conclusion of a Washington businessman, who is the father of an eight-year-old boy.

His boy's hall of gods, he reports, begins with Glenn and Shepard, for whom he has named his two pet turtles. The third hero is Abraham Lincoln; and his fourth, J. Edgar Hoover. The most recent addition to this pantheon, the businessman reports, is Boris Karloff.

The boy has become fascinated with old horror movies and, to his parent's embarrassment, likes to expound before company on the relative acting talents of Karloff, Lon Chaney Jr., and Bela Lugosi. He insists that Karloff is the world's outstanding actor.

The other day, the story goes, the boy announced that he intended to write to Karloff. "Going to tell him you think he's a better actor than Lon Chaney?" his father asked. "No," said the boy, "I don't want to embarrass Lon Chaney."

The exchange was forgotten until, a few days later, the father found the following letter in his son's spelling book:

"Dear Boris Karloff: I am going to watch 'The Bride of Frankenstein' because it is the best. If you don't need your Frankenstein suit any more, can I have it? And if you do need it, just keep it."

The father is worried. His heroes, he said, were Jack Dempsey, Lindbergh, Knute Rockne, Gary Cooper, Lou Gehrig, Tom Mix and Melvin Purvis, the G-man who shot John Dillinger. The present hero shortage, he fears, is creating a socio-psychological problem that may become acute when the present generation reaches voting age.

Should he, he wonders, encourage his son to forget Karloff and worship today's athletic heroes, knowing that they will surely hook him on cigarettes?

CONFUSED AND SHAKEN, FROM PANTS

WASHINGTON, *April 1963*—The big news in American culture these days is "pop art." Many culture experts believe it may be a bigger craze than folk singing before the summer is out, and no wonder.

The exhibition which opened here the other day at the Gallery of Modern Art demonstrated that "pop art" is not only more fun than anything since the Keystone Kops, but also an exhilarating tonic for the ego. A lot of people who have been standing around modern art galleries for years feeling scared and bourgeois are going to go away from this show convinced that almost anybody can be an artist.

For example, consider the effect on the viewer of Jim Dine's brooding black study, "Shovel With Long Handle." What Jim did was to take a canvas seven feet long and cover it with black paint. He then took a coal shovel seven feet long and covered that with black paint. Then, he attached the shovel to the canvas!

The viewer's first response is: "I could do that if I had some canvas, a shovel and black paint." He realizes only gradually that it is not so simple as that. The effect of "Shovel With Long Handle," he senses, is dependent upon its subtle relationship to two other Dine works in the same room.

These are "Black Bathroom"—a sink stuck on canvas on which a good bit of black paint has been indiscriminately smeared around—and "Black Window." The latter, as its title suggests, is a black window—sill, sash, frame and glass—to which several pieces of hardware are audaciously attached at the top. These include an ax, pliers, a wrench, a can opener, an egg beater and a carving knife.

In a different vein, there is George Brecht's "Stool." Brecht has taken a stool and placed a bag of oranges on it. The gallery has arranged matters so that the viewer comes to "Stool" immediately after the emotional shock of Claes Oldenburg's "Pants." This is an oversize pair of bright blue men's trousers made of sailcloth and hung on an outsized clothes hanger.

One moves, confused and shaken, from "Pants" to the cool serenity of "Stool," with its bag of oranges, and finds himself subtly led to reminiscences about oranges he has seen on stools in other times, other places.

The viewer moves with continuing pleasure through a constant series of surprises. Here, for example, is "Starchief," by Robert Watts. It is a green dashboard from a Pontiac Starchief. Plugged into an electric outlet, it makes monotonous noises while its odometer clicks off the miles at a rate which indicates the thing is supposed to be moving at 300 miles per hour.

And here is Robert Rauschenberg's "Black Market," a big rectangle of canvas on which the artist has placed a bedspring, a 1959 Ohio license plate, four metal-jacketed notebooks on which the public may express itself, and a one-way street sign with a dog leash dangling from the arrow tip.

The leash leads to a box on the floor containing a green comb, several yellow pencils, some inking pads and stamps, and the car repair bill of one C. V. West for brake work by the Temple Motor Company of Alexandria, Va. The bill was $53.60. Among the public expressions recorded in the notebooks this weekend was one stating, "Rauschenberg, you are mad."

In an essay for the exhibit program, Alan R. Solomon takes a very somber view of all this, arguing that it has something to do with the fact that modern man "sees himself in his art . . . as a disrupted, contorted victim of the modern cataclysm, torn by forces of a magnitude beyond his comprehension, a grim figure, full of despair and anguish, entirely without hope."

This may be so, but if it is why does the visitor leave the exhibition feeling relaxed, pleased and full of interior giggles?

If "pop art" catches on with the public, as it very well may, American cellars will soon become the scene of more welding and sawing and hammering and soldering than at any time since the do-it-yourself craze subsided. And it won't be contorted victims of cataclysm stripping the hardware stores, but a bunch of optimists pursuing the will-o-the-wisp of art.

AMERICAN DIPLOMACY

Gentlemen, the State Department has invited you to this seminar as part of our new program for assisting all diplomats from the newer nations toward a clearer understanding of the American way of life.

Today, as you know, the American football season is opening and, hence, our discussion will deal with this peculiarly American sport which, we understand, has baffled a number of you. And now we will entertain questions from around the table.

Q. Is this not the briefing for the group which is to visit Disneyland next week?

A. No, Mr. Ambassador. I am sorry, but we are not briefing on Disneyland today. We would be delighted, however, to clear up any questions you might have about football, the great fall sport which so exemplifies the American spirit. Yes, Your Excellency?

Q. I have heard much in my country about the great fall classic to decide the championship of the world. Would you explain, please, why no country but America is allowed to participate in the fall classic since the championship of the world is said to be at issue?

A. I think you will find, sir, that the fall classic is a baseball event rather than football. Baseball, or the national pastime as we call it, is played with a solid, round, white sphere, often called the pellet or the old horsehide. The players dress like little boys in knickerbocker pants and beanie caps, and chew bubble gum. Football, on the other hand, is played with an inflatable prolate spheroid, often called the pigskin. The players wear leather armor and cut off their hair. The football season culminates in a New Year's Day classic, or bowl.

Q. I have read the magazines and sports pages quite thoroughly in preparation for today's discussion, and I note that though no games have yet been played these publications have already selected the ten best football teams and chosen the country's eleven finest players. Why, then, is it necessary to play any games at all, particularly since I am told that the sport is quite dangerous and keeps many young men from their studies?

A. Americans play for the love of the game, Mr. Ambassador. The important thing is not whether you win, but how you play the game. In this way the coaches teach leadership, responsibility and the value of teamwork. They are molders of men. Yes?

Q. Is it not true that this molding process is highly discriminatory in that most of the gentlemen who receive its benefits are from the highly developed, industrial state of Pennsylvania?

A. We have found, sir, that young men from Pennsylvania are peculiarly well adapted for the physical rigors of football. However, our coaches stand ready to mold men of all regions, regardless of race, religion, color or state of origin. The only questions are: Do they have heart? Have they come to play?

Q. Last year, I had the honor to attend a football contest featuring the Washington Redskins—

A. Well, sir, not everybody would call that football.

Q. Nevertheless, I found it most difficult to grasp the moral principle informing the referee's decisions. For example, huge men repeatedly flung themselves beastlike upon a much smaller man who was holding the prolate spheroid. Yet the referee made no protest.

A. That, Mr. Ambassador, is called playing the game.

Q. Yes. The smaller man obviously had much heart and had come to play, for even despite repeated buffetings he finally escaped his tormentors and ran for the score. The referee, however, was incensed and refused to recognize the score. I was told that it could not be counted because one of the huge, beastlike men had moved when he should have been standing still. Would you explain, please, the moral principle on which the referee acted?

A. Well, you see, by moving before the play had started, the big man gave an unfair advantage to the ball carrier. He was, as we say, offside.

Q. But didn't the huge men who repeatedly abused the smaller man also have an unfair advantage of superior weight?

A. Ah, but the smaller man knew that the rules would not protect him because of his lightness, you see.

Q. Are you saying that this great fall sport which so exemplifies the American spirit discriminates in favor of huge, beastlike men? (General commotion.)

A. Gentlemen, gentlemen, please. I can understand your distress but let me note, if you will, that in any reports you may make to your Governments it would be incorrect to describe football as the national pastime. The national pastime, gentlemen, is baseball. Let us never forget it. Young men in knickerbockers. Beanie caps. Bubble gum. And now, perhaps we should bring this to a close while we are all perfectly clear on the distinction between the pigskin and the old horsehide. Thank you for coming.

THE SUBVERSIVE CHAIR

WASHINGTON, *May, 1963*—The sidewalk cafés are beginning to appear for the season here. They are unhappy places, even the one operated by the button-eyed little

Frenchman who wears a flower in his lapel and drifts among the patrons asking judgment on his food.

There are physical reasons for the failure of the sidewalk café in Washington—and in all of Anglo-Saxon America, for that matter. For one, America has not produced a chair suitable for sidewalk-café sitting.

Such a chair, as every business failure in Europe knows, must be of wicker construction with the back tilted ever so subtly to encourage surrender from shoulder to hip. The seat must be deep enough to carry the entire load of the thigh. When sagged into, this chair must produce an inner serenity relieving the mind of niggling worries about time and economics.

This chair, which America cannot produce, is made in abundance in France and Italy. Americans will not import it. It would be too dangerous. As an Illinois Republican once confided while contemplating Lac Leman from such a chair one long idle afternoon in Geneva, "This chair is un-American."

What most domestic cafés use instead is an American chair of chrome and plastic. Its design was perfected in the underground nightclubs that used to line 52d Street in Manhattan. The goal there was a seat that would occupy no more space than an ash tray. It also had to be uncomfortable enough to work the customer into a state of fatigued irritability, in which he would buy drinks at a rapid clip.

The result was a chair now widely used in bus-depot grills, to discourage derelicts from loitering. On this chair, everything a sidewalk café should inspire—languor, the impulse to write a quatrain, the urge to master the conjugation of Persian verbs, decisions to chuck it all and go south—all this is out of the question.

This honest American chair's irascible chrome fights against the body's sag with equal and opposite metallic reaction. It is a chair designed for listening to saxophones on, in dark cellars before dawn, but not for sitting on in the May air and feeling clocks run down in the sunlight.

Look at the miserable café sitter on this chair: His coffee

has a topping powder of red dust windborne from the neighboring crater where tractors and power shovels dig the latest real-estate speculation. An evil waitress uses a dozen cunning devices to humiliate the dawdler into leaving. Who would be foolish enough to ask her for another coffee? Would the manager summon the police if asked for stationery and ink?

There is a compulsion to gulp, pay, overtip and step briskly off to business, all frowns about gross national product and Pathet Lao. Here is a state precisely the opposite of what sidewalk-café sitting should induce.

There is also a big picture. What we are dealing with is another instance of the trouble resulting from the creeping Europeanization of America. In its early stages, the infiltration of Old World culture was limited to institutions easily adaptable to Yankee civilization. Scotch whisky, sports cars. Bullfight posters, tweed toppers. Onionskin weeklies.

Now matters are at the ugly phase. Europe is moving in with stuff that cannot be assimilated by Yankees. The Volkswagen is a case. It is a superb car for a people at ease in leather pants. Americans feel ridiculous in leather pants; it is not surprising that, squatted behind their Volkswagen wheels, they so often succumb to lethal delusions of mobility in traffic.

Another evil Europeanism is the Italian suit. Already, in some shops, a man may have to get ugly to avoid encasement in Italian skin-tights.

The sidewalk café is not a menace like the Volkswagen, or a monstrosity like the Italian suit sewed on the well-beefed American male. It is a humane way of life, but simply not ours. In most cases here, it is just the 52d Street cellar hauled out into the sunlight.

ON WITH THE TEARS

April, 1963—Memo to all candidates for Academy Awards tomorrow night:

In the event you should be announced the winner of the Oscar in your category, you will be expected to appear before the television camera and accept the award with appropriate remarks or gestures. Over the years, our Oscar winners have behaved at this difficult moment with a style that has been a credit to the industry.

We are confident that you will uphold the tradition tomorrow night. Remember, the remarks and gestures you make will be seen in millions of American homes. Strive for humility in the image you project. Avoid arrogance, flippancy and meanness of spirit.

Upon receiving your Oscar, you may feel like looking around the room, sneering at the audience and saying, "You all tried to cut my throat, but I won it anyhow." Emotionally satisfying as this might be, it can only be disastrous for your career. Your whole attitude should convey a single message to the American movie fan: "I don't deserve it." If possible, weep happily a little bit.

Actually, it would be better if the weeping were confined to the more important stars. If cartoon animators and choreographers and set designers and short-subject scenario writers all start weeping, it's going to slow down the show and we've had complaints about its dragging for the past couple of years.

What should you say if you win an Oscar? There are three basic speech themes: (1) Weep happily and say that you don't deserve the award but will accept it on behalf of your co-workers who made everything possible. (2) Weep happily and say that you don't deserve the award but will accept it in memory of your mother who made everything possible. (3)

Weep happily and say you don't deserve the award but will accept it in the name of your artistic forebears who made everything possible.

Suppose you are an actor who has portrayed a character from life. In this case, there are opportunities for interesting variations from the basic speech line. A very favorable impression may be made by saying, for example, that you don't deserve the award but will accept it in the name of Lawrence of Arabia, who made it all possible.

On the other hand, there are situations where this same variation would be graceless. You would not, for example, want to accept the Oscar in the name of Moses or Solomon or the Queen of Sheba. If honored for your portrayal of Moses, Solomon or the Queen of Sheba, it is probably safest to accept on behalf of your mother.

Some artists prefer to do something a little different, and this is fine. It gives the show a change of pace. A favorite device over the years has been to go charmingly inarticulate when the Oscar is presented. A shriek conveying unutterable delight is often adequate for a young female star. Really big lady stars, however, are expected to speak, preferably a message that plucks the heartstrings. It may be advisable to consult a writer.

Well-known male stars may find the casual—but—sincere acceptance fits their style. Come on camera chewing gum and tugging at your nose; get off a mild joke saying that the Oscar is a mere bauble in your book of values; then shift mood quickly by exuding sincerity and saying something earnest like, "I guess if you all really knew just how much this means to me—well—I just can't tell you how—" Weep right here and make a quick exit brushing at eyes.

Above all, no joking acceptances! In the view of the American movie fan anyone who would joke about receiving an Oscar would profane a shrine. Jokers lack humility. They are arrogant, flippant and mean of spirit. What's more, they usually do not get nominated for the Academy Award a second time.

And now, time is getting short. Decide how to accept your Oscar and start practicing. Master a humble demeanor. Brush up on the art of weeping happily. Remember, the critics may prefer Swedes and Frenchmen and Italians, but there will be a lot of people out there to whom you are the only true gods. Weep it up for them.

SHADES OF DISTINCTION

June, 1963—It is pure coincidence that the cosmetic industry's hush-hush Project Dermachrome has been scheduled for this summer when the hue of an individual's skin is such an explosive issue in the country.

The cosmetic barons who ordered it are extremely sensitive to the dangers to which they have exposed themselves, and those few willing to discuss the project at all insist that their motivations are entirely commercial. Their only goal, they say, is to learn what color the white man really wants to be.

They believe that with the advanced state of cosmetics today they can give America a product that will enable every white man to appear in his community without feelings of financial inferiority or social inadequacy.

As one suntan-lotion tycoon puts it, "everybody has known for years that there's no such thing as a 'white' man, in the strictest sense of the adjective. About the closest thing you get to a white man in this society is the off-white man, and he's the absolute bottom of the social ladder—the office worker with only a two-week vacation, the convict, the all-night disk jockey."

It is established social fact that the off-white people are looked down upon by the tan people, particularly in winter. In summer, impecunious, low-status, off-white people may sneak into a distinguished coat of tan by lying on a cheap towel in the yard, but a winter tan separates class from working class.

There are extremely subtle shadings of suntan. The ideal

lies somewhere between the color of a well-kept clay tennis court and a rosé wine.

Sociologists have found that anything darker is frowned upon in genteel circles. Those leathery mahogany hides favored by so many ladies of the Riviera and Miami Beach, for example, are generally regarded as evidence of decadent attitudes toward public service.

Social studies show that the lowest order of suntan is the one shot through with sunburn red. It invariably betrays an off-white with social pretensions. Nothing is more contemptible than the peeling nose, which invariably gives the game away.

A powder-base magnate, discussing the need for a cosmetic application that would disguise nose-skin peelings, says privately that he believes this to be the greatest source of emotional antipathy between tan-whites and off-whites today.

"I confess," he said recently, "that I am willing to treat the off-whites as if they knew Bermuda as well as I do until I see those peeling noses. Then I feel all my old prejudices welling up."

One of Project Dermachrome's main goals is to discover whether the tan skin is losing its cachet. There has always been a type of society beauty who believes that a lovely skin should be kept under parasols in hot weather.

These girls, who grow in rich profusion in northern Europe, have transparent skins with the palest tints of peach and cherry glowing beneath the surface. Their coloration drives men insane and makes the ginger-tan women look like stevedores.

Another extremely desirable color, particularly among men, is baby pink. It is commonly found among Senators of the United States, bishops, bankers and special Presidential emissaries. It is a glowing pink such as might be produced by brisk pinching and many steaming towels.

Actually, it is produced by high dividend pressure. It is scientific fact that no poor man can become a baby pink; that the baby pinks never tan, no matter how often they go to the sun; and that they never become off-whites unless they lose their money.

In later life, they usually become scarlet and finally purple, but whatever shade of life they may be in, they are invariably made way for everywhere as the authentic rulers of the world. Sometimes they may seem to be sympathetic to the tans and the off-whites and the pale-peaches, but they don't understand, not really. How could they?

THE BIG WHEEL

Press conference. "Ladies and gentlemen, the Big Wheel of the United States."

"Thank you. Please be bucket-seated. We'll go right to questions."

Q. Will you tell us, Mr. Wheel, why you have not opened these press conferences to live television? Is it, as some have said, because you are uncertain how well your image will project to the American motorist through this vital medium?

A. No. The fact is that I am still waiting for delivery on a late 1964 image, and as soon as it comes through I will start projecting it. As you know, I had been using an old 1963 image that didn't have much pickup and burnt a lot of oil. My wife has taken that one and I have the new one on order. Let me add that the Wheel intends to cooperate fully with the vital medium in the struggle against peace of mind.

Q. On that point, sir, your war-on-beauty program has hit a snag in California where the Concrete Corps wants to wipe out the redwoods for an expressway. How do you answer these Peace-of-Mind Marchers who say that the redwoods are more valuable than limited-access concrete?

A. I can only regret that many decent, respectable motorists have let themselves fall dupes to the Peace-of-Mind movement. These trees they are talking about are 2,000 years old. Why, that's as obsolete as the Model T. The Peace-of-Mind Marchers talk about sitting under the redwoods and listening to the rustle of eternity. Nonsense. America must move wheels. The motorist doesn't want to hear the rustle of eternity. He wants to meet it head-on at 70 miles an hour.

Q. Are you at all worried about these charges that your war-on-beauty program is turning the country into a junkyard?

A. That is sheer propaganda inspired by the Anti-Mobilists.

Q. You deny the "junkyard" charge categorically?

A. Gentlemen, in a country that must move wheels, a certain mechanical effluvium is inevitable and I regret it. I would be delighted if these millions of useless old cars could be flushed into the rivers and forgotten, but the rivers are already overloaded with household and industrial garbage. Let's face the facts—this is the greatest garbage-producing nation in history. Our great garbage productivity is a symbol of our strength and we ought to think of it with pride rather than shame. America must move wheels to prevent its enemies from closing the garbage gap.

Q. Sir, there are reports that you have been reviewing the urban destroyal program. Can you confirm this?

A. Yes. I have had the Great Paver go over the program and we have decided that there are several cities that will not have to be totally covered with concrete. Here in Washington, for example, we have decided not to take expressways directly through the Lincoln Memorial and the Capitol. We will go under the Memorial and across the Capitol lawn. We felt that while the American motorist wants to move wheels he would prefer to have a few inspirational landmarks standing on the horizons to remind him of the glories of mobilism.

Q. Your opponents in the coming election, sir, are charging that you have lost untold millions to pedestrianism by not pressing guerrilla action against subversive builders who are still, in many cases, laying sidewalks—

A. My opponents should realize that this is a very difficult war, and we fight it in many ways. Sometimes we have policemen stop infiltrators caught on the sidewalks after dusk.

Sometimes we condition children to taunt playmates seen walking the sidewalks to schools or stores. Yes?

Q. Sir, why must America move wheels?

A. Because this world is filling up with unpleasant people who envy us and want to take over this country. We want these people to say, "America—it's a wonderful place to drive, but I wouldn't want to stop there."

PART 2

PEOPLE

JOSEPH VALACHI

What is original in Joseph Valachi's account of life in the big mobs is the picture of how thoroughly the gangsters have aped the middle-class code of modern business organization.

Everyone talks a professional gobbledygook, worries about his status with the boss and professes absolute loyalty to the team. At Christmas, sub-bosses get together with their staffs over a festive turkey. There is even a despised class—the "greaseballs"—who give all other gangsters somebody to vilify while idling in the prison washroom.

Today's gangster does not call his organization a "team," of course, but a "family." The big boss of Valachi's family is Vito Genovese, who happened to be at the Atlanta Penitentiary when Valachi went down to serve twenty years.

The modern gangster goes to prison the way an efficient corporation executive goes to Bermuda. He does not abandon his work; he merely changes his operating base to more relaxed surroundings. Valachi had hardly unpacked before Genovese invited him to come live in the boss's cell.

Valachi's response was that of every organization man ever invited to week-end with the boss. "I told him, 'If you want me to come, I'll come,' " Valachi testified. "How can I say no to him?"

The Atlanta management was apparently giving Genovese the big-guest treatment, for Valachi was promptly moved into his boss's quarters. For Valachi, it meant an ulcerous strain. He obviously lacks the canniness and savoir-faire needed for survival in an executive suite. "I had so much respect for Genovese that sometimes I stuttered when I talked to him," he confessed.

What happened then must seem sadly familiar to every anxious failing businessman who has sat under the boss's nose and watched his sales charts fall. Before long, Valachi was noting "a pretty mean look" in the boss's eye. When a "greaseball," one Vito Aquecci, asked him for "an appointment" to see Genovese, Valachi immediately suspected a plot to ruin him.

In the mob, of course, you don't just walk up to a boss on the prison bocce court and start talking; you get "an appointment." Valachi agonized about what would happen to him if he should set this appointment up for Aquecci and what would happen to him if he didn't. After all, Genovese had a large staff with him at Atlanta—Trigger Mike, Johnny Dio, etc.—and they were certain to find out if Valachi became too zealous about the boss's privacy.

Worry piled on worry. One day Genovese called Valachi over to the executive cot and said, "You buy a barrel of apples and sometimes one of these apples is touched and has to be removed." This is the mob way of telling a man to pull up his socks. There is only one warning more ominous. That is when the boss grabs your hands and kisses you.

In the mobs, a kiss from the boss is tantamount to arriving at the office one morning and finding your rug gone. When Valachi got the kiss and noted that Johnny Dio was oddly anxious to have him step into the privacy of the showers, Valachi concluded that he was "a dead duck" and defected.

What bothers him most, it seems, is not that the organization life is stifling or unwholesome. He was offended when Senator Javits likened his trade to crime. Crime, he seemed to feel, was too harsh a word for a struggling entrepreneur.

He had only had some slot machines, some horses, some numbers action, and, during the war, a $150,000 trade in stolen ration stamps. The only thing he had ever done for the family was "just go out and kill for them."

No. What clearly bothers him is not the organization's work, but Genovese's conduct in office. Genovese made "a big mistake" in ordering an execution in prison, he insists. "Power went to his head," he charges. What's more, he feels, Genovese lacks grace. "He's the tightest guy around."

And finally, he contends that the big boss respects neither legality nor tradition, but passes out death sentences without due process and talks mob business in the presence of "a guy that isn't even a member." "If I did that," Valachi said, "I'd have to run out of the cell."

There is Valachi's indictment. Genovese is incompetent, tyrannical and a disgrace to the highest office in the organization.

BILL SHAKESPEARE

Why we wouldn't have to celebrate Shakespeare's 400th birthday this spring if the sixteenth century had been kinder to people of talent:

Dead memories stirred in many an aging theater buff last week with the news that William Shakespeare, once hailed as the boy genius of the theater, is now earning $10,000 an hour as the largest single stockholder in Elizabethan Tel. & Tel.

Virtually unknown to the present generation of theatergoers and all but forgotten by the old-timers who once hailed his *Henry VI, Richard III* and *Titus Andronicus* as first crude flowers of a budding genius, Bill Shakespeare is now a suave, sixtyish coupon clipper who still turns out an occasional sonnet for his grandchildren but no longer talks about writing "the big one."

"The theater has been good to me," he said over tea aboard his yacht the other day, "but after *Titus* won the Pulitzer, I found myself in such demand that I never seemed to have time to sit down and write the big one."

In the first flush of success it seemed that there would be

plenty of time to get around to the big one, which the critics anticipated would establish him as the peer of Christopher Marlowe and Tennessee Williams. Shakespeare discussed it once in an old *Time* cover story.

"It will be a royal drama," he said, "of murder, revenge and madness." The critics pointed out that these were the themes of *Richard III* and protested that he was planning to repeat himself. "It is now time," one contemporary critic wrote, "for Shakespeare to come out of the royal charnel house and deal with reality—with emasculated men and frustrated women defeated by the futility of life."

Fearful of outraging the critics, the young Shakespeare put his pen aside and surrendered to success. Ed Sullivan snapped him up for three appearances in which he did burlesques of the Plantagenet kings.

His flair for casual banter led inevitably to a series of guest appearances on the Jack Paar show. There he offended the court by telling naughty anecdotes about the Earl of Essex and established himself as such a controversial "personality" that C.B.S. put him under contract to do amusing ninety-second commentaries on the news of the day.

His lecture fee zoomed to $2,500 per appearance. Money began piling up from endorsements of beard waxes, fountain pens and encyclopedias. A newspaper syndicate gave him a rich three-year contract to write five columns a week.

When Warner Brothers purchased screen rights to *Titus Andronicus,* Bill Shakespeare was signed to do the screen adaptation and two original scripts. Always fond of high life, he took immediately to California's swimming-pool society and made no objection when the studio rewrote *Titus* as a Doris Day musical with Rock Hudson in the title role.

The original screenplays never materialized. The other day Bill recalled with a chuckle how he had written a scenario titled "King Lear" about "a blind monarch and some rather ugly daughters." "It was full of poetry," he said. "Blank verse, believe it or not."

The Hollywood idyll ended when Shakespeare's tax accountant persuaded him that the best way to reduce the tax bite on his huge writing income was to quit writing and go into real estate. As Shakespeare's real-estate empire expanded, he gradually dropped from public view, bought castles in Scotland and Italy and began playing the stock market.

"For the longest while," he said, "I couldn't get the idea of doing the big one out of my system. I would sit around writing lines like, 'To be or not to be,' and ' 'Tis not so deep as a well, nor so wide as a church door,' but it was hard recapturing the music after all those lectures and swimming-pool chitchat.

"And of course, taxwise there was no percentage in it. I was always a businessman first, even in the old days at the Globe Theater."

Bill Shakespeare feels that the world has lost nothing from his pen's long stillness. "Truth is," he says, "that I probably never had a big one in me."

LINCOLN AT HOME

SPRINGFIELD, ILL.—It has been more than a century now since Lincoln made his last trip from Springfield, and the town has changed a mite.

The politicians around the state capitol have switched from stovepipe hats and frock coats to two-button suits and shell-rimmed glasses. The legacy of Henry Ford, still undreamed of when Lincoln sadly commended the townspeople to God's care, has filled it with stop signs and one-way streets.

Just behind Lincoln's old back yard Jimmy Hoffa's boys now push their heavy rigs along Route 66 toward Chicago and St. Louis. Night and day, around the clock, the snarl of the tractor-trailer's tormented gear box is heard in the room where Abe sought tranquillity, and plumes of Diesel smoke drift across the wilting petunias in the back garden.

All this, of course, is evidence of the vitality of the Union a century after Fort Sumter and, as such, perhaps it is more fitting than any monument Springfield could build to Lincoln. And yet, what Springfield contributes most vividly to the Lincoln story is the healthy reminder that he was, after all, a man of merely human dimensions who lived a relatively ordinary life in a relatively ordinary town.

Perhaps the growth of the Lincoln legend has done him a disservice by accustoming us all to think of him in heroic terms. In the American imagination he seems to loom Bunyanesque and superhuman, a figure ideally proportioned for and ideally housed in the vast Greek temple in Washington. Springfield and the lush rolling Lincoln country around it help to leaven the myth. They force us to realize that he was built on the human scale and that the extraordinary quality about him was within.

In this way, Springfield does him honor. Superman, after all, is ultimately just a bore going about his daily routine. The human being who rises to the extraordinary testifies to the noble mystery of man.

The best antidote to the mythical Lincoln is his house here on South Eighth Street. It was the only house he ever owned, a tan clapboard two-story structure with dark green shutters, resting on a brick foundation. For those who see him enshrined in the Lincoln Memorial, it is a shock to walk in the front door and discover that it is a house that no modern account executive would visit friends in.

Though undoubtedly comfortable by 1850 housing standards, it would cramp a modern family man with growing boys. The narrow center hall holds Lincoln's original coat rack, adorned with a black stovepipe hat and a shawl. What a racket the children must have raised in there while Abe was trying to think in the rear sitting room.

To the left of the hallway are front and rear sitting rooms divided by a wide arch. Together, they offer less space than the modern workingman's suburban split-level playroom. When the delegation from the 1860 Republican Convention arrived in Springfield to notify Lincoln of his nomination, he stood in the arch to receive them. Standing there now, one realizes that the place must have seemed unbearably crowded, with politicians packed against the small horsehair sofa and Abe's head nearly touching the top of the arch.

This is a house in which Coolidge or McKinley might have fitted to perfection, but it requires some severe adjustments to the imagination to see Lincoln fitted into it comfortably. In fact, it is necessary for the imagination to shrink him down to human size.

And yet, there is every evidence that he lived here comfortably, prosperously and happily, at ease in ordinary human dimensions. Lincoln testified to that in 1861 when he stood on the rear platform of the train that was to take him to Washington and, with the gray drizzle falling around him, said his good-by to Springfield. Besides speaking his affection for the town, however, his farewell also revealed how the man had developed since arriving from the backwoods village of New Salem in 1837 to practice law.

"To this place and the kindness of these people, I owe everything," he said. "Here I have lived a quarter of a century, and have passed from a young to an old man. Here my children have been born, and one is buried. I now leave, not knowing when or whether ever I may return, with a task before me greater than that which rested upon Washington. Without the assistance of that Divine Being, who ever attended him, I cannot succeed. With that assistance I cannot fail. Trusting in Him who can go with me, and remain with you, and be everywhere for good, let us confidently hope that all will yet be well. To His care commending you, as I hope in your prayers you will commend me, I bid you an affectionate farewell."

Now, in Washington where Stanton finally commended him to the ages, he seems too big for life. Here in Springfield, with the big tractors rumbling past the Lincoln back yard and the tourists cramped tightly into the front sitting room, it is easier to see him as a man. This way he seems more wondrous, but also more comfortable.

THE EISENHOWER IN KABUL

WASHINGTON, *September, 1963*—It is good to have the King of Afghanistan in town. His is a sensible visit. There is time for both ceremony and diplomacy, and later he will go sightseeing to Cape Canaveral and Disneyland. Kings know how to do this sort of thing right.

An American President once went to Afghanistan, and the trip was ridiculous. He allotted Afghanistan four hours around lunchtime between state visits to Pakistan and India, cramming it into his itinerary like an anchovy in a ham and cheese sandwich.

The visit occurred in December, 1959. The guest was President Eisenhower. There is still mystery about what happened, and no wonder. The Presidential contingent was in a state between exhaustion and hysteria when the visit began, and everything came unhinged somewhere between the Valley of Roses and the Valley of Cannon, well before the party reached Kabul.

The Afghans have learned the hard way how to deal with great powers. Over the ages they have been trampled over and through by Mongols, Persians, Greeks, Tartars and Moguls, all of whom have used Afghanistan as the gateway to India. It must have been clear to them, from the moment Eisenhower landed, that the American press party was going to be another such nuisance.

Accordingly, the press group was cunningly cut off from the official delegation. The President was put into a fast car and sped along the 38-mile road to Kabul. The reporters were shown politely to buses—exceedingly slow buses, as it developed—and left sitting while every car in Afghanistan raced away behind the President.

The bus drivers seemed decent enough. They smiled fraternally at the worst possible abuse and chattered with delight when someone was finally found to explain to them, in pidgin Persian, that they were supposed to drive these very buses into the capital city.

By the time the buses had clanked off down a valley of inexpressible beauty, all was lost. The Government had somehow gotten word through the hills that everyone was to come down and see Eisenhower, and the roadside was lined for miles.

A cynic later explained over coffee at Chilstoon Palace that very few of these people knew what an Eisenhower was, though everyone knew it was something very important.

Many obviously thought that the press buses were the funny part of an Eisenhower, for they waited patiently for the buses to creak by and laughed gaily at the creatures inside the barred windows. Camels smirked and ugly desperadoes in turbans jumped with glee.

When the stragglers reached Kabul, there was a dense mass of people, camels, oxen and carts, all amassed in the streets to celebrate the Eisenhower's arrival. The President had long since been whisked into the palace, and outside all was revelry and chaos.

A solicitous Afghan led the newsmen into a palace reception room and soothed them with coffee. There had never been such crowds, he said. They should have seen the adulation accorded the President. Premier Khrushchev, who had been here a short time before, had not received half the ovation. He showed the more dyspeptic where they could buy souvenir postage stamps and postcards, a service especially provided for the Western press.

Everybody got off three or four postcards with handsome stamps. A rumor went around that the President had been seen somewhere in the vicinity, but before a general investigation could take place everyone was ordered back into the buses to catch the plane for India.

At the bus door there were mimeographed copies of a communiqué purporting to reveal what the President had talked about. It said that the President admired Afghanistan and wanted to see it get on. It had been composed several weeks before.

Everybody clanked back to the airport and went to India for dinner. It was reassuring to see the President again at New Delhi. U. E. Baughman, then head of the Secret Service, later wrote that the President was overcome by the altitude at Kabul and had to be given oxygen. Who knows? Kings make more sensible tourists.

GENE TUNNEY

August, 1962—Gene Tunney, the pugilist who declined to become a pug, has lent his Maine summer house to the President this weekend, and romance loses again. Old prize-fighters are supposed to end up talking to themselves on the skid-row curbstone, and it is an affront to American myth for Tunney to be doing favors for Presidents.

The sports fans have never quite forgiven Tunney for getting rich in the ring and living happily ever after. In the Nineteen Thirties, long after he had twice whipped Dempsey and retired undefeated, it was still considered faintly scandalous that he had refused to go on fighting until he was pounded into imbecility. On the drugstore corner, where the sporting set congregated in those days, his second victory over Dempsey was dismissed as a freak result of the referee's long count when Dempsey decked him but neglected to go to a neutral corner.

There was always some cynic to note, "Well, Tunney at least was smart; he took his money and got out." But the defense was acknowledgment of the charge—that Tunney somehow had let the fans down, had not played the game. Instead, he banked his $990,000 purse from the second Dempsey fight, married a rich girl, entered fancy society, went to business, took up the classics and offended gymnasium habitués everywhere by turning up at Yale to lecture on Shakespeare.

Tunney's offense was against one of the most cherished myths in the American psyche. "Easy money destroys its finder," goes the cliché, and after "love conquers all" and "straight shooters always win," there are few morals to which the storytellers return more faithfully. Midas turning his daughter to gold, and Sierra Madre prospectors murdering each other for gold dust, old ring champions dying in poverty, Marilyn Monroe destroyed by her own success—all are variations on the same fable.

Tunney made nonsense of the fable, and today little appreciation is wasted on him. Joe Louis, who lost everything, is a more satisfying hero. "Poor old Joe," the saloon philosophers will sigh at the drop of his name. "It's a tragedy." And, "it happens to them all," someone else will observe. This usually builds into a lament for the "tragedy" of Sugar Ray Robinson, of Primo Carnera, of the latest forgotten baseball "immortal" found penniless in a Salvation Army hall.

It is ennobling to be associated with a world so full of "tragedy," even when the association is the tenuous one of onlooker in the bleachers. Tunney, declining to contribute a tragedy to it, tarnished its sad romantic grandeur. He even denied the fans the satisfaction of the traditional comeback attempt, which might have given them the gratification of saying, "They never come back." Once you have said of a man, "They never come back," you have him endearingly catalogued as another of fate's victims.

And now there is the Marilyn Monroe "tragedy." From the first radio bulletins of her death it followed the pattern that had become so familiar in Hollywood "tragedies" since Valentino's death. The inevitable pictures of Miss Monroe's rumpled bed, seen from a peeper's view through the sealed window. The battening flock of sob sisters, the studio publicity man calling it a modern tragedy, the surviving stars grumbling about funeral arrangements, the usual accusations that it was that monstrous abstraction of villainy, Hollywood, that had really destroyed her.

And so on and on in the old pattern calculated to reduce another troubling death to another comforting illustration of the truth of the Midas fable.

The irony of it is that while the ritual harps on the cruelty of fate and circumstance it ends by romanticizing the world that is popularly supposed to be destroying its lovely young people.

As the "tragedy" stories accumulate, they obscure Miss Monroe's human identity and convert her to romantic stereotype, in a class with Valentino, Jean Harlow, Joe Louis and all the other beautiful, fortune-kissed boys and girls who seem to have lived only to prove that the beautiful and fortune-kissed are despised by the gods.

It may be a reassuring myth to those whom fortune has assigned to sit in the bleachers and stand behind the police lines at movie *premières*. Whether it is more than synthetic tragedy is another question.

Gene Tunney, who refused to go along with it, has disappointed the fans and settled for living happily ever after and entertaining the President.

THURMOND WARMS UP

WASHINGTON, *March, 1964*—Senator Strom Thurmond, the undisputed filibuster champion of the world, was going through his first 1964 workout in the Senate the other afternoon.

When the news spread that the champ would be testing his wind, most of his colleagues found inescapable appointments to be elsewhere, and it seemed like a propitious occasion to size him up—to see whether his legs had gone, whether his clichés had rusted since 1957.

In that year, as every *aficionado* remembers, the Senator

denounced a civil rights bill without letup for twenty-four hours and eighteen minutes while standing erect at his desk on the Senate floor, thereby smashing all previous records for pointless oratory. This year, with civil rights again before the Senate, there may be a challenge for the crown.

The South Carolinian has never been a popular champion. The Southerners, who dominate filibustering as the Austrians dominate skiing, have always felt that the 1957 triumph was clearly disreputable, because Thurmond decided to go for the record after the rest of them had promised to keep quiet in return for important concessions in the bill.

The mood of the chamber was properly musty for the Thurmond workout. Galleries were half empty. Ninety-eight of the 100 Senatorial desks were abandoned. From their niches high up in the gallery walls the busts of John C. Calhoun, Thomas Jefferson and Aaron Burr gazed down in marble resignation.

Somewhere outside, the magnolias were blooming and birds were singing in the sunlight, but in here the ancient parchment-colored light falling on mahogany and marble suggested Egyptian tombs and eternity. This is the atmosphere which the filibusterer loves, for it induces a brooding despondency in all who enter. After brief exposure they will accept any settlement merely to escape to light and life.

The champ took up his stance at 12:50 P.M. It was St. Patrick's Day, and he wore a green carnation.

His voice is startlingly thin and high-pitched for a distance talker, and after a while it scrapes the nerves bare. He warmed up with a few routine overstatements, like a boxer testing his jab. The civil rights bill, he said, was a "a man-eating tiger." It would "oppress and subjugate" the Republic. He invoked the "specter" of Reconstruction as "warning to those who would impose arbitrary rule on their own people."

Satisfied that his hair-raising language was in good shape, he settled down to test his stamina. For this, he began reading in a singsong at the rate of about 90 words a minute, like one of those telephone-company automata that tell you the doctor is out and ask you to leave your number.

He chose one of the filibusterer's favorite texts—the inherent inequality of man. It is an obvious argument that few would disagree with—some people have more capacity than others for thriving in this society.

The great filibusterer, however, is not interested in argument; he wants to make his audience beg for mercy. Accordingly, Senator Thurmond recapitulated the history of the phrase, "All men are created equal."

At 1:25 P.M. he was telling what Thomas Jefferson thought about it. And George Mason. And the Adams family. At 1:44 P.M. he was examining where the Texas, Indiana and Florida Constitutions stood.

At 1:51, an hour after his opening, he was analyzing the position taken by the Constitution of Liberia, and as the clock moved toward 3 P.M. he had satisfied himself that "equality" was really an idea peculiar to Communism. At 5:15 he was still at it. In the galleries, nerves screamed quietly. The brain struggled against stupor, succumbed to fantasies of mummies and eternity.

The old champ is in great shape. He may still be talking. It is hard to tell. One has these fantasies and waking is indistinguishable from sleep.

ESTES KEFAUVER, OBIT.

August, 1963—He was an egghead masquerading as a yokel and what he wanted was the Presidency. For six years, with little more than a coonskin cap and the stamina of a drayhorse, he kept the most skillful politicians of the Democratic party in a nightmare.

Up and down the American folkways he plodded with his huge right hand dangling limp before him, ready for deposit in the claw of anyone who crossed his path. He would hand them the hand and look through them and murmur, "Ah'm

Estes Kefauver and Ah'm runnin' for President. Will you he'p me?"

From Harry Truman in the White House down through the bull-roast-and-clambake crowd, the party professionals despised him. He was a maverick.

"Always running for President," his colleagues in the Senate said with an inflection that meant, "he doesn't belong." The Southerners viewed him as a traitor to the cause, a Southerner seduced by ambition into espousal of civil rights and other un-Southern flapdoodle. His TV investigation of the mobs, which had publicized certain ugly facts about the relationship of dirty money and urban politics, had won him the lasting hatred of the big-machine politicians.

Campaigning across the country on a chain of outstretched hands, Kefauver found the opposition of the professionals a boon of sorts. He could say with Liberace, "Nobody loves me but the people." And so, it seemed, the people did. But conventions are purely professional institutions and both times—in 1952 and 1956—the professionals had their revenge.

In 1956 he managed to win the sop of the Vice Presidential nomination, and the professionals assigned him to the obscurity of campaigning in the deep-corn country.

The campaign was a model of disorganization. He fell hours behind schedule, kept audiences waiting until midnight until finally, out of the storm, groggy with fatigue, that distant dreamy look on his face, he would stumble into the hall to be greeted by his dismayed local agent.

"What kind of audience you got here?" he would ask as he moved in his stately stiff walk down the aisle, giving them the hand-flapping motion that passed for a wave. "Indians," his adviser told him one night. "What's their problem?" Kefauver asked. "Damn it, man! They're Indians! Isn't that enough?"

The irony of Kefauver was that the coonskin cap, by which the country at large knew him, was a fraud. It implied a log cabin rustic bred to the cracker barrel circle, but it concealed one of the authentic eggheads of American politics. Behind the homespun façade was an upper-middle-class family background, a university education, a law degree from

Yale, marriage to a cultivated Scottish beauty, and a quality of introspection so deep that he was most enigmatic to those who knew him best.

In the Dixon-Yates affair he was a match for the best minds of Wall Street in the intricacies of high finance. In private conversation he was given to a mordant, ironic humor far deadlier to the politician than Adlai Stevenson's good-humored wit, which was said to have offended the voters.

None of this showed on the public façade. To the country he remained the mountaineer in coonskin, exuding the smell of the old hills. Subconsciously or by design, he exploited the Lincolnesque in his figure and towered among his "little people" as a symbol of all those virtues associated in the national memory with log-cabin roots.

"Will you he'p me?" went the pitch. "I grew up in a little, small town, and I have the same ambitions, the same aspirations that most of you have."

And yet, if the façade was all wrong, there was a germ of essential truth in the coonskin, for he had the backwoodsman's innate distrust of big business and the "interests" and an admirable zest for stepping on rich fat toes.

Those who trailed him on his quest for the Presidency will remember him for a time to come, standing on the old-fashioned bandstands in courthouse squares murmuring, "You'll he'p me, won't you?" And, "If you can't give me your votes, remember me at least in your prayers."

PART 3

THE LOSERS

SHEEP AND GOATS

Richard J. Whalen's absorbing account of "How Joe Kennedy Made His Millions" starts off innocently enough in the familiar rhythms of capitalism's success stories.

There was the starting triumph; in this case, winning control of a small bank. Then the "smart Yankee lawyer" who saw the young Kennedy's potential and pushed him along. Then the job with the inevitable shrewd broker and genius speculator who taught him about fancy investment dealing.

The faithful reader of rags-to-riches fables follows all this with senses quivering, for bitter experience of these tales has taught him that no matter how simply they begin they are eventually going to obscure the one point the reader wants clarified. This is: What is the secret of making millions?

Mr. Whalen's narrative, however, proceeds with unexampled clarity, as these things go. The reader can even use it to jot advisory notes to himself. For example, (1) win control of small bank, (2) get smart corporate lawyer to line up big job, (3) learn investment ropes under genius speculator, and so forth.

Indeed, to this point, the story of how the late President's father did it seems so simple that anyone controlling a small bank to start with could follow his example and make more millions. Then we come to the passage in which Whalen describes Kennedy's maneuvers in the entertainment business. "He immediately established a $500,000 line of credit at four banks that provided ample working capital," Whalen reports.

Here the reader puts down his pencil and tosses his notes

into the fireplace. The account of Kennedy's manipulations becomes increasingly more fascinating, but it is now the fascination of an incomprehensible and unattainable dream world that holds the reader and not the charm of the do-it-yourself blueprint for making millions.

The reader knows there is no point in jotting down among his directions to himself something that says, "(4) immediately establish a $500,000 line of credit at four banks." The average reader does not even know what a line of credit is, but he is fairly certain that if he walked into his bank, went to the teller and said, "I want to establish a $500,000 line of credit immediately," he would be held for the police or psychiatric examination.

The really remarkable thing about Joe Kennedy is that he was the type of man who could walk into four banks, announce that he wanted to establish a $500,000 line of credit immediately and make the tellers say, "Yes, sir!" This is a rare talent that people either are or are not born with. Those who are born with it, like Kennedy, will inevitably become millionaires. Those who aren't will go on reading how other men made their millions without ever mastering the essential art.

Everyone knows how to spot the men cut out for really big money successes. They are always sitting around in big leather chairs talking about establishing lines of credit and joking about the price of gold in London and saying, "Merger is the only thing that can save Consolidated." When they go to the bank, the bank dick himself opens the door for them.

The man who is not born with these characteristics cannot really hope to acquire them, no matter how closely he studies the success stories of the millionaires. Try as he may, he will never quite grasp the distinction between establishing a line of credit and opening a charge account.

At lunch with important people, whom he wants to impress, he either becomes too timid to say something like, "Merger is the only thing that can save Consolidated," or he gets it off with such apologetic insincerity that important people dismiss him as a lightweight.

When he goes to the bank, the bank dick does not open

the door for him. Quite the contrary. The bank dick watches him carefully as he reaches for a pen. In really bad moments, the nonsuccess type may find himself holding the pen up grinningly for the bank dick's inspection to show that it is not a weapon.

In some cases, it requires an act of raw courage for the nonsuccess to face the teller with a demand for $25 from his own bank account. Suppose the teller should snarl at him about disturbing the bank's equilibrium! The thought of what might happen if he strode up to the bank dick and asked for immediate establishment of a line of credit is too humiliating to dwell upon.

For this fellow there is no great mystery about how the Joe Kennedys of the world make their millions. They are blessed at birth with a rare immunity from the common affliction we all know as "bank tremens."

ENVIRONMENT EXTRAPOLATOR WANTED

There was a "Help Wanted" ad in the newspaper for a senior vibration analyst. He was needed to establish a mathematical system for determining vibration environments of launch vehicles, and the small type of the ad read as follows: "Responsibilities call for airborne application of advanced techniques in shock, vibration and reliability analysis, involving extrapolation of environment from individual components in the launch vehicle to still more advanced vehicles now in design stages."

This is the kind of thing that makes the mid-twentieth century such a difficult age to love. It is depressing to think of all the desperate job hunters who must have stumbled into this ad for a vibration analyst and felt the will to fight on drained out of them with the realization that enterprise is no longer enough.

Not too many years ago a hungry man with wit, gall and negligible experience could fake his way into a good many of the positions he saw offered in the newspapers. "Sure I can work a three-whelk lathe," the average man could bluff, knowing that he had a sporting chance to learn from watching the man at the next lathe, or from breaking the machine and watching the machinist repair it, if only he could get into the shop.

It is ridiculous to think of this same man nowadays saying, "Sure I can analyze vibration," or, "Give me a chance and I'll extrapolate environment from individual components in the launch vehicle to still more advanced vehicles the way you've never seen environment extrapolated before."

It is impossible. He does not even know what a vibration analyst is. A mathematician claims that he knows, but says it can only be explained in Greek symbols, and not in English.

"But there is no need to explain what one is," he says, "because if you are a vibration analyst, you know what you are." This would not be so discouraging if it were an isolated case, but it is not. The papers are full of such offerings.

Here is one for a man experienced in "analysis, synthesis and design of digital logic for application to computer-directed automatic checkout systems." Here is another for people experienced in "digital systems/data handling, RF systems, GSE, servo-design, antenna 'hat' design and pad electrical systems," and in "solid state analog/digital circuitry," "real-time data processing" and "waveform analysis."

It seems to be impossible to get work of any sort nowadays without experience in "systems." What are "systems"? The ads refer to "system proposals," "unmanned systems," "future systems," "systems employing offensive weapons in space," "systems decisions," "land systems," "major system building blocks," and "target systems."

"Systems men," says a typical help-wanted ad, "when you work on a system at Mitre you think in terms of subsystems that could be a far-flung sensor network. . . ."

"What Does a Systems Engineer Do at Hughes?" asks another ad, but the answer is little help: "Determine systems requirements for manned airborne electronic systems and supporting ground equipment to carry out necessary technical direction to assure system integrity."

It is indeed wonderful, as our happier oracles remind us, that we live in an age when some men can think in terms of sub-systems that could be a far-flung sensor network, and know what they are thinking about. These, in fact, may very well be the people who will represent us at our best in history.

No hero is a total blessing, however. This new one also symbolizes, unhappily, the inevitable twentieth-century defeat of the unfortunate and the unschooled. " 'Sure,' I said, 'I know how to fling a sub-system across a sensor network,' but a machine just laughed at me."

Our hero also has a defect. Practically none of us understands a word he says.

ONE JUMP BEHIND

October, 1962—Why did they have to give John Steinbeck the Nobel Prize? Steinbeck was out, finished, kaput. "Steinbeck just won't do," the supreme court of American letters had ruled in the late nineteen-forties, after finding his work appallingly innocent of Kierkegaard, Proust and Longinus.

For all those who loved the Joads and all their kin it was a cruel ruling, but we accepted it like loyal Americans confronted with a distasteful change in fashion. In the most conspicuous stretch of the living room bookshelf, Steinbeck's works were obediently integrated with Faulkner's and, to show we were aware of existentialism, with Kafka's and Sartre's.

Over the years, "Tortilla Flat," "In Dubious Battle" and "The Grapes of Wrath" were gradually demoted to the out-of-sight shelves upstairs with "Studs Lonigan," "The Secret Diary of Harold L. Ickes" and "Penrod and Sam." Now, with the Nobel Prize, Steinbeck will once again be in. Once again, we will have to dust off the Joads, display them in the living room and relearn to liken their flight from Oklahoma to the Book of Exodus.

This is the kind of experience that has made the modern American such a wary animal over the last quarter century. Somebody is always changing the code of values on him. When Longfellow and Tennyson went out of fashion, they stayed out of fashion. Now, in just twenty-five years, we have had Steinbeck in, out, and in again. A man can't know whose opinion of Steinbeck he should cling to. It's almost enough to make him form an opinion of his own.

These treacherous shifts in literary fashion, of course, endanger only a comparative minority. The man who insisted that Steinbeck was a fine writer during his out period was scorned only in literary circles. But think of the millions who are trapped each year in unfashionable tastes in cars, politics and entertainment.

The typical victim is usually the sensitive, well-informed person making a conscientious effort to stay in step with his times. Perhaps because he spends so much time studying the trends, he is always a step behind them, always finding that the fashion he adopted this morning went out of style yesterday afternoon.

He is the man who bought tail fins when everyone else in the subdivision was buying sports cars. He had just caught up with gin and tonic when fashion was dictating vodka. By the time he learned that the silents were the only movies worth seeing, they were being shown to the masses on television and were out. When he finally got to Paris, he discovered that the smart people were going to Rome, and when he finally got to Rome, they were all going to Mexico.

He bought hi-fi the year that stereo came out and switched to king-sized filters when the pacesetters were going back to unfiltered short cigarettes. He gave up television to show his contempt for the wasteland just when the critics were discovering Ernie Kovacs.

When he finally knew enough about the missile gap to discuss it, the Democrats were saying it didn't exist. Embittered by a lifetime of being right too late, he has become one of life's losers. He cheered when Senators Dodd, Keating and Capehart demanded a tough policy toward Cuba, only to find that the opinion makers supported President Kennedy in a cautious policy toward Cuba.

To stay in the best company, he studied the opinion makers and had just discovered that Cuba was a secondary threat not worth fighting about when Mr. Kennedy proclaimed it a menace to peace that had to be removed even at the risk of war. It would be pleasant to think that after this final disappointment he sat down with Steinbeck's book, "Travels With Charley," and that after he finished it he said to his wife: "Steinbeck is wonderful. He's taken me on a vicarious trip across America."

He did, in fact, sit down with "Travels With Charley." We do not know exactly what he said to his wife but, knowing our man, we can assume that it went something like this:

"Steinbeck is pleasant, but he'll never win any prizes as a great writer."

Could there be a conspiracy somewhere against us?

TRAILING CLOUDS OF DUST

One of the unwritten membership rules of the American ruling class is that traveling by train between New York and Washington is cause for expulsion.

Fear of flying is occasionally accepted as an alibi, but even in these cases the membership review board is apt to ask why the violator couldn't have made the journey by automobile. It is unclear why the ruling class has rejected the Pennsylvania Railroad, which is now the only line handling passengers between here and New York, but none of the popular theories is really persuasive.

All that is certain is that the influential minority that gets results in this country has forsaken the rails almost completely for the flying machine. This is a pity, particularly on the Pennsylvania's New York-to-Washington run, which could be one of the nation's premier passenger services if the ruling class used it, and which is one of the nation's dreariest because the ruling class ignores it.

What we get from our betters, when they consider railroads at all, is a lot of cosmic talk about the railroads' "plight," full of knowledgeable stuff about featherbedding, tax handicaps and discriminatory subsidies. This may be all very well, but most of it has an unconvincing quality, which may be explained by the fact that the advisers' personal experience of railroads consists largely of looking down on them from airplanes.

What the ruling class ought to do is get down out of the air and get a taste of life on the rails between New York and Washington.

How else can they understand the unutterable gloom that descends on the traveler boarding the typical passenger coach? The paint is peeling from the ceiling. The windows surely haven't been washed since the second Cleveland Administration. Layers of gummy soot lie petrifying in the corners of the window sills.

The floor is a litter of dead cigarette butts and old candy wrappers that crunch underfoot where the dirt is dry and stick to the soles in passages where spilled coffee, milk or fruit juices are still damp.

The unyielding seat cushions exhale clouds of ancient dust as they receive the traveler's weight. After a while the dust resettles in the pores of his face, clogs his nostrils, sifts along his cuticles. The primitive heating system starts to work; the traveler begins to perspire; he can feel the dust turning into minute mud balls and trickling in tiny rivulets down his temples; the heat is cruel.

There is the diner with its promise of anesthesia from the bar. First, a stop at the washroom to blot the dust. The washroom turns out to be a tiny evil closet. The soap dispenser is broken, the water is not quite hot. The light is dim, ghastly . . .

The walk through the long string of coaches is an adventure in odors. Temperatures vary wildly from coach to coach. In this one, passengers huddle under their topcoats; in the next, men in shirtsleeves, ties loosened, doze glassy-eyed in tropical heat.

The diner is a haven. Someone has thoughtlessly furnished it with comfortable chairs, clean white tablecloths, freshly polished silverware. Hasn't it occurred to the Pennsy that it has a bungler loose somewhere in its dining car division?

The trouble here is that strange couples are forced to eat side by side, devising conversation suitable for being eavesdropped on by other strangers. And it is painfully clear that most are painfully aware that they are not really, truly, ruling class.

They talk in loud desperation of irrevocable trusts that they mean to set up tomorrow, of the thousand shares forgotten in Aunt Louise's box at the bank, of incredible successes in sales engineering, of everything, in short that they conceive to be the conversational chaff of the ruling class.

The real ruling classmen, of course, are riding comfortably 15,000 feet overhead talking about the plight of the railroads. "We've got to ameliorate these discriminatory subsidies to ease the tax handicaps on featherbedding, or the railroads are dead."

And then, the long walk back to the home coach, and the awful scene with the conductor when he catches you without your ticket, which you left back with your luggage. Mercifully, he decides not to have you jailed in Trenton. It is the prevalence of such courtesies that keeps the railroad passengers from revolting.

THE DEAD-WIRE GAMBIT

When success arrives it is followed two weeks later by a secretary. The secretary sits at a desk outside the door looking efficient, forbidding and protective.

Almost at once, she turns success into a problem. It would look bad to let her just sit there buffing her nails. She must be given work to do so that everyone can see that success is no bed of roses. It must also be impressed upon her that she is working for a man who counts for something.

American business culture has evolved several ways for dealing with these problems. One way is to give the secretary plenty of dictation. The standard practice is to call her in and dictate a dozen letters to important men whose names will awe her.

For example: "Dear Walter, You have rung the bell again with this morning's column, which I read aloud to my wife over breakfast. I was reminded of something Richelieu once said when confronted with a similar situation during the . . ."

Or: "Take a letter to John Steinbeck. 'Dear John, Just a note to tell you that I have been re-reading Tortilla Flat with the kids and . . .' " Walter and John may resent a total stranger's addressing them by their first names but, being gentlemen, they are unlikely to reply snappishly. Moreover, the letters will make work for their secretaries and, thus, lighten the drain on their own creative energies.

Once a success has impressed his secretary with his importance, she will be on guard against common nuisances who want to waste her employer's valuable time. The problem here is to persuade some common nuisances to come to the office so the secretary can throw them out. Encyclopedia salesmen are very useful for this purpose.

The problem about making an appointment for someone to come in so he can be turned away is that the secretary will insist on making the telephone call. A success who makes his own telephone calls rarely makes it all the way to the board room.

In fact, one of the first duties of success is to waste other people's time by making them hang on a dead telephone receiver. Everyone knows how this works. The phone rings. A feminine voice says, "Mr. Sterling?" "This is Sterling speaking." "Will you hold on, please, for Mr. Success?" The line goes dead while Sterling holds on.

Nine chances out of ten, Sterling has never heard of Mr. Success, but he is curious to find out who he is. It is unthinkable for a man with a secretary to call Sterling directly. For one thing, Sterling himself may have a secretary, in which case she will humiliate him by saying that her man is in conference. Secretaries have little respect for men who make their own phone calls.

The common practice is to have the secretary place four or five calls, asking each party to hold on, and then go to the water cooler for a chat with the office boy. This lets all the people holding dead receivers understand where they stand in the cosmic order.

It is not clear why success must have everyone wait on it at the telephone. If a successful man were going to call personally on someone, he would not send his secretary ahead to ask his host to drop everything and sit tight for the arrival of Mr. Success. If he did, the host would tell her to take a flying leap at the switchboard.

Some people, of course, have no phone manners at all. When asked, "Will you hold on, please, for Mr. Success?" They say, "No," and hang up. Fortunately for the man with a secretary to keep busy, these are a small minority.

It is apparent from all this why so few successes ever go on to do great things in life. The job of making work for their secretaries takes everything out of them before they move up to their first oil painting on the office wall.

UNHINGED IN A CRAMPED PLACE

The newest thing in neurosis goes by the medical name of *numerophrenia gravis* or, to use the layman's term, "digit dudgeon."

The symptoms are an abrupt rise in blood pressure, a deep red flush, an alarming increase in the pulse rate and violent hand movements. The victim may clench and unclench his hands spasmodically or strike out with fist at inanimate objects—desks, tables, chairs, telephone directories.

As he loses self-control, he goes irrational and commits unspeakable rudenesses. In the aftermath, he becomes morose, brooding, apologetic and loses the capacity to think young.

Over a prolonged period, the patient slowly comes unhinged. He loses his will for a vice-presidency, dwells morbidly on "the good old days," starts carping about his electronic society and concocting juvenile plots to humiliate computers. It is a short step to disemployment and a quart of 69-cent sherry behind the pawn shop on Skid Row.

J. B., a typical *numerophrenia gravis* case, tells of his own ordeal in these words: "It has now reached the point where I want a drink every time I reach for the phone. To call home from the office, I have to remember an eight-digit number sequence. Long distance means eleven digits. One wrong digit and I'm ruined.

"I tell myself, 'You can do it, J. B.' But every call is a test. I reach for the phone and catch myself thinking, 'Suppose I can't cut the mustard any more.'

"Even when I get through on the first try, I'm wrought up,

curt, bad-tempered and rude. Sometimes I forget what I'm phoning to talk about."

J. B. experienced his first seizure two years ago while trying to make a credit-card call to Baltimore from a pay booth on the New Jersey Turnpike outside New Brunswick. The call required him to dial O (for Operator), recite his credit-card number (021-7219-B18), the Baltimore code (301) and the number of the phone he wanted rung (964-7385)—a sequence of twenty digits and one letter.

He had run through the first fourteen or fifteen digits flawlessly, as he tells it, when some memory link snapped and he began reciting his Social Security number. On the second try, he blurted out his driver's permit number when he should have given his credit-card number, and was informed that his card was out of date and that he would have to pay coin for the call.

When J. B.'s wife finally found him, he was trying to tear the phone from the booth. The family doctor reminded him that he was no longer a boy and advised him to start golfing on weekends.

A prudent man, J. B. decided never to be caught off-guard again. He kept pocket notebooks which he filled with the accumulating numbers he needed to survive—phone numbers, credit-card numbers, ZIP codes, license numbers, insurance-policy numbers, V.A. numbers, club numbers, passport numbers, payroll account numbers, library card numbers, safe-deposit box numbers, Blue Cross numbers, charge account numbers, etc.

Friends began smiling behind his back and calling him "Old Lumpypockets." He finally sought professional care when, after trying to deposit some money one day at his bank, the teller demanded his account number.

Until that instant, J. B. had never realized that he had an account number. He was calmed by a vice president with the aid of the bank dick.

Fortunately, J. B. has an enlightened employer who realizes that "digit dudgeon" is not a vice, but an environmental disease of the age, like smoker's hack and overkill tic. His wife and employer are extending him the understanding he will need to get through to retirement age. Unfortunately, there is no cure.

Like all the hidden sufferers of "digit dudgeon," J. B. is simply obsolete. Evolution will ultimately replace all these sluggards with a new race bred to make life happier for computers.

What a pity that J. B. will not be around to admire the marvelous life that the machines will create for man—one of these days.

AL THE NOBODY

The income tax would be tolerable if the Government would give us an explicit accounting of what our money is used for.

At present this is impossible to get. Suppose Al Brown calls Washington and says, "I am Al Brown of 721 Green Street, Oshkosh, Wisconsin, and I want to know how you used the $927.18 I paid you in taxes last year." Eventually, he will be connected with a voice at tax headquarters which will tell him that 60 cents of every dollar is spent on the military, that so many cents are spent on education, so many on illuminating the Capitol dome, and so on.

These figures are not of the slightest interest to Brown. He wants to know what his $927.18 was used for, and it would make him a better citizen if the Government would tell him. The Government, for reasons of its own, will not tell him.

These reasons are very interesting. Suppose the government looked it up and told Brown that his $927.18 had been used to print ten pages of the Congressional Record (at the going cost of $90 per page). Even without knowing Brown, one can imagine his reaction. It might be necessary to collect his next tax bill at gunpoint.

However, Brown would probably resign himself to supporting the Congressional Record and start reading it to see what he was getting for his money. Before long Brown would probably be at the Capitol with a huge committee of citizens whose taxes pay for the Congressional Record, and this huge committee would probably want to know, rather testily, just what had been going on there for the last 175 years.

What happens, in short, is that Brown, given a tangible responsibility in Government, snaps out of his civic lethargy and becomes an alert citizen. It is exciting to think of what might result from a precise tax accounting to every citizen.

Naturally there would be some resistance from pacifists whose money is used for war goods, Negroes whose money is used for subsidizing Mississippi and John Birchers whose money goes to the U.N. On balance, however, the argument is overwhelming for giving every citizen an accurate report.

The weakness of the present system was dramatized in a small incident at the Capitol recently when some misguided tourist took a snapshot inside the empty House of Representatives. A lady tour guide interrupted her speech and began screaming for the police, who came puffing up, laid hands on the tourist and seized his film.

There are regulations against photographing the House Chamber. (What if such pictures reached the hands of the Chinese Communists?) Still, in a Government where every citizen was sure of his importance, a small rule infraction would hardly have ended in public humiliation.

The tourist in Washington tells himself that this is his city and these his buildings, but in his soul he cannot believe it, and in the suspicious gaze of the White House cops and in the Capitol signs telling him to "keep out" of Congressional preserves, he is warned that he had better not try making himself at home.

Al Brown realizes that when his $927.18 is split proportionately among all Federal activities, he is not contributing enough to anything to cut the least bit of ice in Washington.

The policeman who seizes his film knows that Brown feels like a nobody and, of course, there is nobody that governments, politicians and policemen enjoy pushing around more than a nobody.

But let Brown know the truth—that he is the man who buys Senator Dirksen's cigarettes, who helped pay for the President's dinner last night, or who owns a piece of a nuclear submarine somewhere in the Arctic—let Brown know this, and you make him a menace to government.

He will get nasty with policemen who try to seize his film, insist that Congressmen quit doctoring the record, tell the F.B.I. to get off his telephone. He will quickly begin feeling himself the equal of governments.

Governments nowadays are too cunning to put up with much of that. That is why nobody will tell Brown what was done with his $927.18. Poor Brown. Look! The Government is opening a secret dossier on Brown now. The Government knows a menace when it sees one.

WHY RISE AND SHINE?

The American alarm-clock industry is circulating a long treatise on sleep. It contains ridiculous advice on how to take the agony out of getting up.

For example: "The average sleeper goes through three steps in waking up: (1) the period of awakening when the alarm rings, (2) the period of relapse when the sleeper plays possum with himself, and (3) the period of re-awakening when the sleeper wakes himself up all over again. . . . The second period is the trap—and one to avoid, by getting up at the first sound of the alarm."

Many people, of course, can get up at the first sound of the alarm without bad results, but these are not the kind of people who really enjoy sleep. They snatch it on the run, regarding it as a necessary impediment to dynamic living. People who are not so luckily constituted should take care.

These people, upon responding to the first sound of the

alarm, invariably wind up before the medicine-chest mirror, swollen-eyed and creaky, seeing themselves and their lives with brutal clarity. In bad cases, they go back to bed and never leave it again.

There was a typical case some years ago in Newark, N.J. A normal, undynamic young man named Arthur, who dreamed of some day becoming president of his company (this was before young men lowered their goals to vice-presidencies), got up at the first sound of the alarm and sprang to his bathroom mirror.

There, with his normal waking illusions still dormant, he suddenly glimpsed himself as he was—sallow, unprepossessing, watery-eyed, slow-witted about business. In a fearful flash of truth, he saw quite clearly that the presidency to which he aspired would go to the boss's nephew and that he would be retired at seventy with a platform rocker.

Arthur went back to bed and took up reading the classics. Relatives took him in, and he became something of an authority on Italian Renaissance poetry and a drag on the economy. Had he not insisted on hopping out of bed one morning at the first sound of the alarm, he might have enjoyed the life of a normal, self-sustaining taxpayer and be retired today with a platform rocker.

The alarm-clock industry also has this advice for difficult wakers: "Give yourself an important job to do soon after arising (taking out the garbage, lighting the stove, etc.). This makes sure you get up."

The point here, obviously, is that waking with a sense of mission will help sleep lovers to get past that awful moment before the mirror when intimations of mortality crowd in. Taking out the garbage and lighting the stove, however, will not do the trick.

Most men who wake up thinking, "I must rise and take out the garbage," will immediately go back to sleep thinking, "Garbage, schmarbage." What is needed is a truly important reason for getting up, and here is the rub.

The time to decide on an important reason for getting up is just before retiring at night. "I need an important reason for getting up tomorrow morning," a man may tell his wife. In most families there will probably be a blank exchange of stares. The wife will want to say, "The important reason for getting up is to get out and make the mortgage money."

A smart wife will not say this. She knows it will start that old rondelay which begins, "Is that all I have to live for?" It will occur to the husband that perhaps there is no important reason why he should get up tomorrow. He may brood.

In any case, there has been raised a question between them that should remain unasked. In extreme cases the husband may refuse ever to get up again until his wife gives him an important reason for it. And if she tells him the truth—about the mortgage money—they may both end at the marriage counselor's.

The alarm-clock people should forgo the advice and concentrate on producing the irresistible alarm clock. It should flood the room with sunshine collected from a childhood morning in June and give off the scent of wild roses.

In a no-nonsense feminine voice, it should evoke a zest to grab life by a leg and pish-tush all those gloomy suspicions that a foot put out of bed is merely a foot set on a treadmill.

REFINANCE YOUR MIND

Here is something new for everybody to worry about. It is a new sociological concept called "poorthink." People who fall into the "poorthink" category should probably re-examine their lives while there is still time.

"Poorthink" is a social condition marked by chronic or persistent refusal to behave like a millionaire. The person so afflicted is commonly said to "think poor." One of the airlines, in a campaign to sell its first-class seats, is already demonstrating the great potential of the "poorthink" concept for advertising.

The airline's TV commercial presents a well-tailored, purring man, who never talks to anyone but the most vital people. Those cheap old coach and tourist seats may be all right for some people, he winks, oozing contempt for all of life's losers. But no man of consequence, he goes on, can expect to "think poor" in transit, then get off the plane and think "like a vice president."

This is probably the first persuasive argument ever made for the first-class airplane seat. After all, who wants to feel like a grits-and-hog-jowls mentality when for $25 extra he can fly across the country thinking like a vice president?

The boon to advertising and consumption should be generous. Thousands of consumer articles just as useless as first-class airplane seats may be sold not because they bestow any status or enhance the buyer's sex appeal, but because not buying them would leave people feeling poor and, hence, alienated from the national mainstream.

Nobody wants to be classified in the "poorthink" group these days, not even the poor. Newspaper reporters who periodically rediscover the poverty of West Virginia invariably get a bale of angry letters from West Virginians protesting that there has been too much written about poverty there and demanding recognition of the state's wealth and assets. The assumption seems to be that if the rest of the country would stop "thinking poor" about West Virginia, things would automatically start to improve.

It hasn't been so long ago that "poorthink" was the heroic attitude for all American youth who wanted to get on. Work hard, shoot straight, don't squander your money on frivolities like Popsicles, girls who kiss on the first date and first-class airplane seats—and life will bring its rewards. So went the myth.

Everybody knew it was a myth, but it was bad form to say so. Social usage required everyone to carry on as though straight shooters really did always win and as though hard work and pure living really did lead to the pot of gold. Children were taught the virtues of thinking poor and left to cope as best they could with the slow discovery that the meek, humble and upright were on an impecunious path.

There is not much of this left nowadays. If there is an unquestionable moral to be drawn from the Bobby Baker affair, it is that the way for a young man to make $2.2 million is to ingratiate himself with rich and influential people. The country is swarming, of course, with people who would rather be caught short at the bank than be seen in last year's car.

Family solvency is not yet a felony, but many economists consider it vaguely unpatriotic. Even President Johnson's insistence on turning off the White House lights is widely regarded as a stunt to pacify "poorthink" remnants that remain in the country. Smart people know that if his example is widely followed, the utilities and light-bulb manufacturers will soon be at the Capitol for Federal relief.

With the formulation of the "poorthink" concept, we are entering an era where a full set of status symbols will no longer be enough to get a man by with his neighbors and boss. "There's that clod, Carrothers," they will say of him. "Oh, I know, he has a Mercedes, two-and-a-half children in private school and a Vassar wife, but he eats domestic cheese and chipped beef at lunch."

"Thinks poor, does he?" "You can always spot them. There's a certain something," "Too bad." And another little death will have quietly occurred.

PART 4

THE WHEELED PEOPLE

HAPPY BIRTHDAY, MACHINE

This is the birthday of the machine that moved the world. It was a tough, plain, black oblong box mounted on wheels and it cost $850. Henry Ford called it the Model T.

Nowadays it is fashionable to lament the passing of the Model T, even among those too young ever to have had to cope with it. As it has receded deeper into memory it has acquired the simple grandeur of American myth. Detroit doesn't build them like that anymore, no sir.

Of course Detroit doesn't. The Model T was built for a nation of farmers. What Henry Ford had in mind was a car the farmer could afford. It was to be an all-purpose machine that could take a farmer to market, saw the wood, pump the water and do the churning.

Ford's genius was in building it cheaply enough. Before that, the automobile had been a rich man's toy; the Model T, at $850, became part of the American household. Ford put the country on wheels. And what countrymen do when they get on wheels, as the subsequent history proved, is go to the city.

In the city, the farmer soon learned that wheels alone were not enough. He wanted white sidewall tires and a rumble seat and flower vases beside the windows. And so the Model T was actually a self-destroying machine built to transport the farmer into a world where he could discover that the Model T life was not for him.

Much of the nostalgia that now attaches to Ford's 1908 car is probably not for the old Tin Lizzie herself but for the lost transitional era she typified—the time when the family still had roots in the soil, sent the children walking four miles to school, rattle-banded newlyweds on their wedding nights, went to sewing bees and looked on a ten-mile trip as an overland journey.

The practice of abusing Detroit for not giving us a modern counterpart of the Model T ignores the fact that today's mighty wheelorama is designed on the same basic principle. It is an all-purpose machine for the city dweller. In time our children may look back on it with the same affection we feel for the Tin Lizzie and may adopt it as a nostalgic symbol of the good old days of the mid-twentieth century.

Just as the Model T was designed to make life easier around the farm, the cars on the market now are built to make life easier around the cities. Thus, the hand crank that was needed to start the Model T has been replaced by the automatic starter. The reason is clear to everyone who can remember the extraordinary proportion of male motorists with broken arms during the Model T years. Nowadays women have to use the car two dozen times a day to meet the complex demands of urban life, and this is a country that doesn't like to see its women's arms broken.

For contemporary man, who may spend 10 per cent of his life in his machine commuting, the modern car provides music, news and traffic bulletins. In hot weather, it cools him with air-conditioning. In cold, it bathes him in warm air. Deep upholstered cushions ease the discomfort of sitting long hours each month in jammed city traffic. Great blinding tail lights help protect him from dangerous drivers to his rear.

Tinted windshield glass shades his eyes from the glare of neon. Push-button controls for the windows, power steering and automatic transmission all help conserve his strength for the city's exhausting business luncheons. Bucket seats tell the thousands around him, who would otherwise not know, that he is a man of significance in the community.

What will the sentimentalists of the early twenty-first century make of all this? Will it remind them of the beautiful lost past when the family had its roots in the city and mother drove the children four blocks to school and the world was a simple place with only the old-fashioned hydrogen bomb to worry about?

No predictions today. They would seem too frivolous, and frivolity is not fitting when we hail the birthday of the Model T. It is more appropriate to get into the wheelorama and drive to the country and note how quiet it is now where the old farm communities used to stand.

THE PASSING ORDER

The automobiles are getting restless. They may already be composing a declaration of independence from human control and drawing up charters of internal-combustion rights.

Research conducted recently along 618 miles of turnpikes clearly indicates that something sinister is in the wind. It is clear that the automobiles are beginning to respond to laws of their own and that there is very little that their drivers can do to stop them.

Consider the curiously inexorable law governing turnpike passing, which the machines obey with blind compulsion. This is known among experimentalists in machine psychology as the Passing Order. With the triumph of the turnpikes, it is possible to demonstrate that a Passing Order not only exists, but also governs the behavior of automobiles with ruthless firmness.

It is the basic principle of the Passing Order that all cars produced last year must pass all cars of the same make produced this year. There is no mercy for those that violate the law. If a 1963 Chevrolet, for example, refuses to pass a 1964 Chevrolet, all the other cars laugh at it until it either passes the new car or retires to an ignominious career of Sunday motoring.

The reasons why 1963 models must pass 1964 models are fairly well understood. Being slightly out of fashion, they must compensate for their feelings of inferiority by demonstrating that they can still whip any car on the road.

Why do the 1964 models let themselves be passed? They have the serene contentment of richly turned out women who are aware of their superiority. They feel it would be bad taste to go zigzagging down the turnpikes like fading movie stars. Moreover, they want to be admired by other cars and they are afraid of getting dents in their new grilles.

There is no human reason, of course, for any car to pass another on the turnpikes. The new roads are so engineered that all cars can easily maintain the same high speed and the same distance intervals. It is now possible for 10,000 cars to travel from Newcastle, Del., to Boston without ever changing their relative positions, yet the cars reject this human discipline.

The complexities of the Passing Order are only vaguely understood. It is well known that little cars must pass big cars and that old cars must pass new cars, but age and size are by no means the only factors at work.

For example, big cars occupied by politicians must pass everything. Cars built in 1950 or before are not expected to pass anything, unless they have no front fenders, need repainting and have two exhaust pipes, in which case they must pass everything except cars containing politicians.

If an old car with two exhaust pipes lets a car with a big aerial pass, all other cars must accelerate and pass the old car with loud laughter. The old car must then leave the turnpike and buy new spark plugs.

Equally poignant is the problem of the sports car. The sports car is allowed to cruise at a reasonable speed until it spots a group of other cars bunched dangerously close together.

Then the sports car must race up to the cluster, locate the tightest space between cars and cut into it, thus demonstrating its amazing brakes and agility. There are hundreds of other refinements. There is the awful compulsion upon Oldsmobiles and Pontiacs to overtake Greyhound buses. There is the lethal obligation placed upon convertibles with squirrel tails flying from radio aerials. The machine psychologists have only the vaguest grasp of how the Passing Order governs these curious phenomena.

One thing seems reasonably certain. People ought to think seriously about getting out of these automobiles whenever they reach a turnpike. That's where the cars will strike first if they ever decide to revolt.

GOD'S OWN COUNTRY

LOUISVILLE, KY., *August, 1962*—They have an exciting new idea in highway engineering out here. It is called the low-speed, two-lane, unlimited access road, and to anyone who dreads the drudgery of expressway driving it looks like the wave of the future.

For one thing, it is more dangerous than the old-fashioned superhighway. Farmers are forever pulling out of cornfields right across the traveler's bow, and hairpin curves are constantly threatening to send him to Kingdom Come. Giant tractor rigs hurtle past within inches, smacking the car with a shock wave that leaves it shuddering. All this not only appeals to the natural American love of excitement, but also keeps the driver from sinking into the drowsing stupor that makes turnpike driving such a trial.

The real beauty of the low-speed, two-lane, unlimited access road, however, is that it has character, individuality and style that tell the traveler a little something of the variety of America. This is what the superhighways have lost. Except for minor differences in vegetation the New Jersey Turnpike looks exactly like Florida's Sunshine State Parkway, which looks like the Maine Turnpike, which looks like Interstate 95 in New Hampshire, Virginia and North Carolina.

The superhighway is designed for a nation of bypassers. It bypasses the grandeur of Frenchman's Bay, bypasses the magnificence of New York City, bypasses the sprawl of Philadelphia, bypasses the neon of the Florida Gold Coast. When the Federal Interstate Highway System is completed, it will be possible to bypass all of America.

The motorist who is bypassing his country may get to his destination a little faster, but he becomes a traveler who is untraveled. Instead of becoming a richer man, he is reduced to a dozing lump of boredom whose horizon is no broader than the next "rest stop."

The truth is that the superhighway is essentially un-American. The idea was imported from Hitler's Third Reich, which gave the world the *Autobahn.* Hitler's Reich was the ideal country to bypass at seventy miles an hour. This is a good country to examine at slow cruising speed.

There is, for example, the sharp shift in moods that occurs at the Big Sandy River where Route 60 crosses from West Virginia into Kentucky. Behind, to the east, lie the industrial towns of Huntington and Charleston, the steamy summer air of clusters of railroad shops and the ammoniac smell of chemical plants. Back farther still to the east lie the breathtaking Appalachian peaks and river valleys. The traveler whose preconceptions have readied him to find West Virginia a place of poverty and squalor is shocked to find that it is also a place of Swiss beauty and much industrial promotion.

Then, swooping up into the hills of eastern Kentucky, the mood of the road shifts abruptly. Bypassing nothing, it allows time to read the changes in the roadside signs. (Another charming feature of the two-lane road is that signs are posted everywhere to relieve the monotony of the landscape.)

In Virginia the billboards reveal a sharp competitive instinct among cave operators. "World's Only Known Anthodites," boasts a typical cave entrepreneur outside Front Royal. In West Virginia they betray an up-and-at-'em mood. "We Feature the Future," declares the welcome billboard at Ceredo, W. Va. And in eastern Kentucky they announce the beginning of the Bible Belt.

"The New America Needs the Old Faith," advises a

church billboard in Ashland. "God's Bookkeeper Makes No Mistakes," warns another at the center of town. And at Olive Hill there are the Start the Day With God Church, a barn broadside cautioning the traveler to "Make Peace With God" and the Gospel Wheel Bar-B-Que.

Winding westward past the country of crude, unpainted shacks and small tobacco plots, the road flows into the lusher farmland of Shelby County. "Shelby County: Home of Good People, Good Land and Good Living," reads the welcoming sign. And as it moves toward Lexington through the Blue Grass country, the evidence of good land and good living and billboards selling good bourbon tell the tourist how the country around him is changing as he moves west.

For incurable bypassers, it is an exasperating road, full of ill-graded curves, and farmers moving at stately pace and red lights stopping progress in unbypassed hamlets. For those who can take their bypasses or leave them alone, it is a cheering reminder that this is still a country that remains to be discovered by those with the will to explore.

The *Autobahn* with its bypasses may be making it easier to avoid exploration and discovery, but the two-lane, low-speed, unlimited access road is out here, ready and waiting.

THE INSOLENT LOBBIES

It is a law of American life that easy things must be made difficult, and what is happening to the motel in this country illustrates the law at its strangest.

Originally, the motel flourished because it was the motorist's easy alternative to the difficulties of the hotel. It was located outside the central cities, which made for painless access with a car. There was no parking problem, no doorman problem and no bellhop to tip.

You put the car in front of the room door, and there was no difficulty shoving all the luggage and scruffy effluvium of auto travel across a few feet of pavement and into the shelter. It was beautifully easy.

Best of all it eliminated the unpleasantness of the hotel lobby. Every motorist knows about this. A hotel lobby is basically a preening stage for the affluent. Vital men who have just closed big deals stand about with corsaged ladies under the proud scrutiny of the room clerk.

When people who have spent a day in a car step onto this stage, they inevitably subject themselves to laughter and contempt, with their stained clothing, bloodshot eyes and unkempt hair. If they carry a sack of dirty laundry or a bag of decaying banana peels or a bowl containing two small turtles, as many motorists do, the encounter with the room clerk can be an ordeal in humility.

The motel eliminated all this. The man at the desk was usually a lonely soul who was pleased to have a moment's relief from the office TV set. Occasionally, he might invite you into a secret place for a drink. If he saw the turtles at all, he would tell you stories of his own experience with turtles.

This was the motel that boomed in the 1950's as the motorization of the country became absolute and, of course, there are many such places left. In the last few years, however, the inevitable complicating process has begun.

In its new manifestation, the motel has become the motor inn. The country is suddenly sprouting with motor inns. Their appearance in city centers and crossroads everywhere has been one of the most remarkable changes in the national landscape since 1960.

One distinctive characteristic of the motor inn is that it makes motoring more difficult than the motel. For example, it is rarely possible any more to park the car outside the room. Motor inns are usually built on several levels. What's more, many are selling food, liquor and meeting-room space on the side, and this creates a public-parking problem.

As a result, the bellhop is back. Tipping is back. Elevators are back. And the lobby is back, with its vital males and corsaged ladies.

Another distinctive characteristic of the motor inns is their absolute lack of regional character. The huge chains that operate them appear to be building them all from the same blueprint.

Each is like the one last night, with identical furniture, identical plumbing, identical floor plan, identical lighting.

Once inside, with the inevitable traverse curtain closed over the inevitable glass wall and the inevitable air conditioner humming smugly, it is difficult to remember if this is San Diego, Chicago or Charleston, W. Va.

The final oddity is the success that the motor inns are enjoying in city business centers. Here the separation of traveler and car is just as complete as it was in the unhappy old hotels. And, of course, to reach them the traveler has to fight his way through inner-city traffic. Once there, he confronts all the basic nuisances of hotel living that once drove him to the motels.

What is happening, obviously, is that the motel has turned into a hotel. Once again, the traveler finds that advance reservations are advisable, that bellhops and room clerks are essentials of life, and that dirty laundry and turtles should be kept in concealment.

This is not a whine against the triumph of the motor inn. There is a lot to be said for it. It is just that it's so hard remembering where you are when you get into one of these things. Take this inn here at Springfield—Sorry, this inn here at Birmingham—Say, operator, what state is this?

MEDICAR

If the Republicans were better politicians they would start doing something about the high price of medical care for the car in this country before the Democrats beat them to it.

The garages are overcrowded, the mechanic schools are

not turning out enough repairmen and the costs of garage care have risen since the war to the point where a major breakdown may exhaust the life savings of the victim.

This works the greatest hardship on the 17 million Americans over sixty-five who are living on fixed incomes and cannot buy a new car every two years. The cost of repairing these senior automobiles, cleverly designed to fall apart at the age of three, is often an insupportable burden on the people who can least afford it.

In short, the country looks politically ripe for a medicar program. For the politicians it is a dream issue. There is no American Mechanical Association to threaten medicar backers with punishment at the polls. The old country mechanic who used to come in the middle of the night to examine your coughing carburetor has practically disappeared. With him has gone most of the country's admiration which made the mechanic a respected community pillar whom no politician dared to push around.

In his place there is a new breed of specialists: ignition men who can't repack your front-wheel bearings, brake experts who wouldn't consider looking at your fuel pump, transmission surgeons who think it beneath them to diagnose a rear-end rattle.

When the specialist replaces the general mechanic, costs inevitably go up. Worse than that, the important human relationship between car owner and garage man is destroyed. The wheezing car is no longer an old acquaintance whose breakdown history and personal idiosyncrasies are familiar to the friendly fellow in overalls. Nowadays it is just another chassis waiting on the lot for an engine lobotomy.

The garage man has given way to the superintendent of the service department. His job is to admit the patient, get the next of kin out of the shop without a scene and collect the bill. His manner combines the unction of the undertaker and the aloofness of the medical specialist.

It is as useless to press him for information about the ailment as it is to ask a nurse what your temperature is. Such mysteries are beyond the layman's grasp, and the superintendent of the service department prefers to discuss them on the telephone when the bill is ready.

"Well, the brakes didn't need relining, after all." Good news. "But the lower right ball joint has to be replaced, new front shock absorbers put in, the front end realigned, and you'll have to have a new idler arm. With the grease and oil, that will be—"

"Sixty-three dollars," you say. It is always $63, just as television repairs are always $37.50.

"Sixty-three dollars and thirty-seven cents," he continues. "Including the grease and oil."

This is the fourth time in a year that the idler arm has been replaced. Why do idler arms wear out so rapidly in this particular car? A superior chuckle, full of mysterious knowledge. "They just don't make them like they used to." And those ball joints; a new set of ball joints was put in just four months ago at a cost of $63. What's wrong with the ball-joint system? "Those ball joints are funny things, sometimes."

What are ball joints anyhow? What in the world is an idler arm? The questions go unasked. The old country mechanic would have diagrammed them for you, but how can one betray the depths of his ignorance to the superintendent of the service department?

And so, the $63.37 is paid, and will be paid again and again as the fuel pump quits working, and the head gasket blows, and the ignition switch fails. And as each payment is made, the latent rancor grows in the body politic.

In the hands of demagogues the rancor might be exploited to bring about socialized car care. A good Republican alternative might be a Federal program for training a new generation of old country mechanics.

Admittedly it would involve some Treasury spending, but it would have the virtue of restoring the vital mechanic-motorist relationship. Republicans being Republicans, it is predictable that they will dismiss the idea as frivolous and miss another chance to match the nation's temper in the Sixties.

PART 5

LOOKING FOR AMERICA

DARK HARBOR, ME.

Every place has its crisis nowadays, but the agony of Dark Harbor is unique. What happened, you see, was that one day, a long time ago, the clock here stopped.

The stopping of the clock was hardly noticed at first. Clocks, after all, wear out, run down, refuse to tick, and somebody solves the problem by supplying a new clock. Here, however, it gradually became apparent that the trouble was more profound than that. Time itself had run down.

The precise year that time stopped in Dark Harbor is a matter of dispute. Some believe it was about 1912, when the invention of the income tax forced millionaires to start wondering whether they could afford a private yacht. Others contend that it happened after the 1929 market crash, when the old tycoon-sailors were nearly obliterated and New Dealers began preaching damnation of the Dark Harbor way of life.

In any case, it is very eerie here now in the quiet past. The island sits isolated in the center of Penobscot Bay, linked to the Maine shoreline by a ferry which quits running at sundown. In the evenings, when the fog rolls in and the birds withdraw, the twitching intruder from the twitching America of the 1960's can hear his nerves sigh in the stillness.

This may be very therapeutic for twitchers, but it is hardly calculated to make the islanders happy. The year-round population that once lived tidily by satisfying the whims of the rich in a two-month summer season has now shrunk to a few hundred hardy souls who are beginning to worry about getting time started again.

Each year the number of the very rich who summer on the island becomes smaller and the average stay becomes shorter. In the good old days, whole families arrived en masse for the season. Now the women come and bring the children and grandchildren, but the men get here only for occasional weekends and a couple of weeks' holiday from the money-grubbing.

For the islanders, still dreaming of the era when the harbor was filled with yachts and the whole economy could be mobilized to rush a bunch of hot-house grapes by sea from Bar Harbor for a tycoon's centerpiece, the present state of affairs is both spiritually and economically depressing.

They sit around under the stopped clocks discussing the number of servants attending the rich men's households this season and arguing that something has to be done about Labor Day. The trouble, they tell you, is that everybody leaves at Labor Day. And why? It is a ridiculous custom. After Labor Day there are five or six weeks of good vacation weather left on the island. Now, if the President would just move Labor Day back to the middle of October. . . .

The problem is that the vacation business in this country no longer rests on the custom of yacht owners. Today's tourist dollar comes from the man with an outboard.

To get into the 1960's, Dark Harbor needs to lure this gross traveler from the mainland. The lure is obvious enough. You promise him Paradise in a gracious place where time has stopped.

The trouble, of course, is that if he comes in sufficient strength, time will start again, as it has at Bar Harbor, where you can hardly get a glimpse of the past any more through the glare of the honky-tonks. This would doubtless be economically sound for the islanders, but it would leave one less island in the world where a refugee from twitching America can stand under the stars and hear his nerves sigh.

The dilemma of the American vacation is that what is good for the vacation business is bad for the vacationer. Somewhere, this country should be able to preserve a few Dark Harbors where the jangling American can ponder the mysterious quiet that was part of his heritage before twitching became the universal civic obligation.

Bad for the vacation business? To be sure. But the islanders will always manage enough to retire to Florida, where they can learn to twitch in harmony with the rest of the country.

BOSTON

October, 1962—It was raining here the other day, a cold, penetrating, misty rain with the dank smell of the North Atlantic on it. A day for communing with the old ghosts who haunt these twisted streets. Conditions were fine—Teddy Kennedy and George Lodge had taken their loudspeakers out of town—and the communing was good.

In the Granary Burial Ground just across the street from Dini's Sea Grill, Sam Adams and John Hancock were resting quietly under the wet green sod. Josiah Franklin and his wife seemed nicely at peace about their boy, Ben, who went down to Philadelphia to get on in the world. Somebody had stuck a single red rose in the soft earth of Paul Revere's grave.

Out of the graveyard and up past Brimstone Corner to Beacon Hill to catch the shade of the late George Apley. Mr. Apley was distinctly present and rather pleased, it seemed, about the bright splash of chrysanthemums and potted geraniums on the front steps of the prim old town houses.

Then down toward the Boston Common, where a stone slab loomed out of the mist, introducing John Winthrop with his words to the first settlers in 1630. "For we must consider that we shall be as a city upon a hill. The eyes of all people are upon us so that if we shall deal falsely with our God in this work we have undertaken, we shall be made a story and a by-word through the world."

The mistake was in reading the monument down to the bottom. There, it announced that John Winthrop's message was being presented by courtesy of the late Mayor James Michael Curley, who, three centuries after Winthrop and before "the eyes of all people," won election from a jail cell.

Curley's shade kept insisting on being heard, and there was nothing to do but give it the time of day. It went like this:

Shade: Nice words by old Winthrop there. Very literary. Of course, I was a literary man myself.

Communer: I know. I read *The Last Hurrah* and saw Spencer Tracy play you in the movie. How do you think John Winthrop would run if he had to get elected in Boston today?

Shade: Winthrop couldn't be elected dogcatcher using that "city upon a hill" line and talking about "the eyes of all the people" being on us. That sounds like Adlai Stevenson. Winthrop would have been a talker. I did some fine talking in my day, of course, but people don't go for it any more. Tell me, boy, Ted Kennedy isn't talking, is he?

Communer: Oh no. Ted doesn't waste much time talking. He is busy shaking people's hands and playing the Teddy Fight Song and having his picture taken with barbers, firemen, policemen and editors.

Shade: That's good. What about Lodge?

Communer: Lodge is trying to talk, but nobody is listening to him.

Shade: Good.

Communer: Of course, Lodge is also shaking people's hands and playing Italian, Polish and American fight songs and having his picture taken with barbers, grocery operators, hamburger stand waiters, envelope factory foremen and editors.

Shade: Well, if he keeps that up he'll at least be able to beat Winthrop. Who are you voting for?

Communer: Can't vote here. I'm from out of state.

Shade: And what brings you to Boston?

Communer: The eyes of all people are upon Boston. The Kennedy-Lodge campaign has been made a story and a byword through the world. The world wants to know if Massachusetts will deal falsely with this work it has undertaken, and I am here to find out.

Shade: Oh? Then I'll have nothing more to say to you, sir. Outsiders who get the voters to thinking about what the world will say of their conduct could be the ruin of Massachusetts politics. Good day.

The mists on the Common were still fine for communing, but Curley's presence had become overpowering and the older ghosts had become sulky. Tom Paine refused to be summoned, and the Redcoats lay still in their graves declining to contribute even a distant musket echo to the scene of the Boston Massacre.

On Tremont Street a sound truck had started up about a Lodge television appearance, and at Kennedy headquarters they were selling records of the Teddy Fight Song.

NEW YORK—I

It must be the eternal hick in all of us that makes us feel ill at ease and bullied in New York. We contemplate a visit here with all the misgivings of rustics about to match wits with the devils of Babylon.

Englishmen have the same provincial qualms about venturing into London. Outlanders of the Augustan empire probably felt the same fears about a visit to Rome, and the ancient Egyptians about a weekend in Thebes.

New Yorkers, naturally, cannot understand why anyone should be put off by their city. It is doubtful if many New Yorkers even realize that these strangers are seething with inner misery, dreading the arrogance of waiters and smarting under the imagined snubs of bellhops.

There is no rational explanation for this, but it is an incontestible fact of American life. Back home, we are all city people nowadays. Still, New York is so firmly embedded in the American memory as the big city that it has a mythical existence which makes the other towns seem commonplace by contrast.

Recently, a new defense has been evolved. You tell yourself that it is not your part of the country that is provincial, but New York. "Most provincial place in America," the going cliché has it. Variations on the theme have it that New York has "lost its charm," "sold its soul" and "let its old spirit die."

And then, "The theater's dying." "Third Avenue is ruined." "Times Square is a honky-tonk." "Central Park after dark is a no man's land." Washington, which has recently been betraying pretensions to urbanity, has begun to tell itself that the great center of American civilization has shifted from the Hudson to the Potomac.

And yet, if this is so, why do we still feel the emotional tug when the sweep of the turnpike suddenly reveals the first distant tracery of delicate gray towers rising through the mist? Why do we strain to find a conversational opening to tell the New Yorker that Washington's National Gallery is really quite a match for the Metropolitan, or that San Francisco is more charming by far, or that he doesn't know what traffic is until he has driven the Los Angeles freeways?

The galling thing is that these revelations rarely disturb the New Yorker at all. Very likely, he will be delighted to hear them, for he rarely envies other towns and is usually pleased to hear that they are doing well. He may even tell you that New York is going to the dogs and cunningly balm your provincial ego by announcing that you are fortunate to be able to live in Chicago or Phoenix or Hagerstown, Md.

The most irritating thing of all is that New Yorkers really don't care what you say about their city. Years of research in this field have turned up only one example of big-city chauvinism worth mentioning. That occurred years ago when a New Yorker, after listening to the conventional catalogue of gripes, finally balked at being told that it was impossible to get a decent martini here. "Why," he exploded, "you can get the best martini in the whole damn world in New York City!"

The outburst was uncharacteristic of the breed. On balance, they are tolerant of the rustic's edgy criticism because they rarely harbor repressed desires to live in Chicago, Washington or Hagerstown and have none of the small-town pride that makes the Chicagoan, the Washingtonian or the Hagerstowner bridle if you suggest that his city is less than the most.

It is this imperturbable New Yorker's confidence in his own town's urbanity that shakes the confidence of the visitor and leaves him seething with small-town envy.

And so, when the bellhop snarls at the tip, as bellhops will everywhere, it is magnified into a symbol of New York ruthlessness. When the clip is applied in a joint, as clips are applied in joints around the world, the victim feels that the city has had him.

It is the hick in him, probably, the part of his soul that has hated cities from the time of Ur. You can't relieve it by telling him that "New York is a summer festival."

NEW YORK—II

Impressions of New York from an outsider's notebook:

Kissing is the thing among smart people here. It is displacing the handshake as the standard form of greeting inside the establishment. At social gatherings women kiss men and women kiss women on entrances and farewells. It is all very Russian, although men are not yet kissing men, at least at the better parties.

The technique of the New York social kiss is ritualistically casual. It would not do for a gentleman to lean into a lady and smack her hungrily on the lips, nor for a lady to do anything that would smear her lipstick on a kissing companion's collar or jewelry.

In a correct kiss, the two parties approach within hand-shaking distance and bow from the hips until they are cheek-to-cheek and lip-to-ear. Then each kisses at the air around the other's ear lobe. Nobody knows why kissing is in. Natives say they have been doing it for the past two years, but don't know why they started.

Rule 1: Men never kiss women on first introduction. Rule 2: Even among friends, men wait for women to initiate kiss. Curious fact: men who give women "I-want-to-be-kissed" stares always have to settle for handshakes.

Horns—This may be the last city on earth where drivers cling to the quaint old belief that traffic will move if honked at loudly enough. Even Paris has given up on the horn, but not New York. Freeze 300 machines in an intersection and all will start wailing threats to smash the others right in their fenders.

They will, too, for New York automobiles are extremely hot blooded. Nothing arouses them like 200 yards of unblocked asphalt dead ahead. With tires, gears and pistons screaming, they leap forward as though on open turnpike to Pittsburgh, then slam to a howling stop at the next light, throwing off tire rubber and hurling bodies around inside.

It will not do to wag a finger at them if nearly run down at a street crossing; they will only lean up against you and nuzzle your hips with their radiators.

Theater—expensive and inaccessible. Except for shows with a death rattle, box offices never have tickets. Ticket agencies usually do—for a substantial added fee. Intermissions create dreadful human strains.

For example: Went to see "Dylan." (Fine play, even at $7.50 per seat, plus $1.50 ticket agent's charge.) Intermission arrived, and with it, problems. Thirsty. Bought half pint of boxed "orangeade" for 40 cents, an overcharge of approximately 800 per cent. Tasted like potash in an acid solution.

Everybody out in alley, smoking, drinking potash, analyzing play furiously. "This is the story of an irresponsible man," observed an indignant young responsible man to his girl. Others expatiating on stage lighting, sets, Alec Guinness's voice, Dylan Thomas's poetry, quality of first-act striptease.

Why does everyone have to stand around for ten minutes loudly missing the point of plays in New York? Answer: When you pay $9 a seat and have a ten-minute intermission, you must persuade yourself and eavesdroppers that you are not only buying an unforgettable experience but are also the type of person who can savor it a full $9 worth.

Some suggestions: Squash "orangeade" sales. Overprint programs with large notice reading: "Relax—$9 is no more than you would pay for an average second-rate meal anywhere in midtown Manhattan."

Building—New Yorkers are always talking about how dull the new buildings are. They are right, but the worst of the new buildings is their coldness. The lobbies of the new hotels and the Pan American Building exhale a chill as from the unopened Pharaonic tombs and in their marble labyrinths there is an evil presence that hates warmth and sunlight.

Regrettable facts: These buildings are not created for people. They are created for real estate speculators. Before long they will cover all Manhattan, and everybody here will go as mad as the automobiles.

NEW YORK—III

The girls of New York come in a glorious assortment of cosmetics and hair styles and sweeten Manhattan with mysterious wisps of perfume.

They are more theatrical than the girls of Washington and less ferocious than the girls of Hollywood, and in their autumn foliage, which is now at its peak, they make Manhattan as spectacular as a ride down the Skyline Drive. For unaccountable reasons, New York tourist promotion has never exploited the natural wonder of its girls, although they are one of its greatest scenic assets.

The night view from the Empire State Building is awesome, but it can't compare with the morning view along Madison Avenue when the girls are arriving for work in their green eyelids and copper hair. At least half the charm of Greenwich Village is created by the girls fighting for emancipation from Ohio, and Fifth Avenue would be a failure without the long-stemmed beauties who have to be pampered in limousines and gossamer and wrapped in fur against the night air.

Many of the city's girls, of course, are not properly New York's own, and this may be why it does not countenance girl-watching as an organized tourist activity. Many are on loan from the rest of the country. When an American girl leaves home to make her fortune and build a family, this is one of the three cities she seriously considers as a promising operations base. The other two are Washington and Los Angeles.

Parents whose girls choose Los Angeles often die of heartbreak. These girls usually wind up hustling cheeseburgers at drive-in restaurants, develop fallen arches, take to sun glasses and marry muscle-builders with too much hair.

The girls who go to Washington are different. Few of them have ever won a beauty contest, if only because they are the kind of girls who think it unsound to be photographed in bathing suits. They have been brought up to believe that the way to a man's heart is his stomach, and this makes them canny. Washington, a city that considers compromise a triumph, makes them cannier.

No Washington girl would come to work wearing green eye shadow like the girls of Madison Avenue. Green eyelids spell hussy in Washington society, whose code is set by the rural Congressional Dixiecrats who govern the city. The girl in green eyelids will end up being investigated as a security risk. If she wants to survive and marry a man with a dispatch case, she must keep her eyes clean, wear unexciting heels and discreet sweaters and learn to ask breathless questions about the Gross National Product.

After dark a Washington girl may wear a wig—the Kennedy ladies wear wigs—but it may get her mentioned in the newspapers next day. The preferred style is unstartling elegance. Downtown she may lug a shopping bag. And, of course, Washington girls who wear sinister black sweaters and insist on emancipation from Ohio are encouraged to go to Greenwich Village.

By comparison, the girls of New York are exhilarating with their heels precariously high and their hair tormented and shellacked. They have the indiscreet quality of girls remembered from early youth.

A boy might smile at them and get a smile instead of the inviolable stare of a girl on guard against security officers in boys' clothing. Their minds doubtless are engaged in immensely subtle schemes involving account executives, theater producers and whiskery philosophers, but it is heartwarming to think that not one in a thousand has ever thought of the Gross National Product.

From the girls of Los Angeles a man expects a cheeseburger served at his car; from the girls of Washington, a stylish companion who would not embarrass him at dinner with a Senator.

There is nothing practical to be said for the girls of New York. They are for smiling at in the struggle against Ohioism, for pampering in furs against the night air and, like the girls of Paris, for watching and for making the city inexplicably more exciting.

DELAWARE TOWNSHIP, N.J.

The authentic American wilderness of the 1960's is not really in the primitive West any longer, but right here in Delaware Township. It is a wilderness of asphalt and exhaust gas, of neon monsters, roadside liquoramas and machines that do eerie things in the night.

This motel room, for example, has a slot machine beside

the bed which, on receiving a quarter, activates machinery attached to the mattress. This is "The Famous Magic Fingers Massaging Assembly." Lie down, insert 25 cents and "it quickly carries you into the land of tingling relaxation and ease."

The children love it, as they love everything about this roadside world. Left to their own impulses, they would use up a month's allowance keeping the magic fingers massaging. Is there something unhealthy in letting children develop a taste for vibrating mattresses? In the old wilderness, they would have reveled in a bed of pine needles, but surely one must change with the times.

The new wilderness, however, is not confined to Delaware Township. It flourishes all along the mid-Atlantic megalopolis in what used to be the rural or small-town areas separating the old cities of Washington, Baltimore, Philadelphia, New York and Boston.

Basically, it is Noplace-on-the-Highway. There are brand-new housing subdivisions along all the ridgelines and valleys, but the landscape is lonely and the atmosphere is heavy with menace. ("Criminal registration required," is the universal greeting sign in this section of Jersey.)

In all parts of the forest, the traveler is constantly harassed by the terrors of an unseen law. Signs warn of awful punishments for committing litter. Everywhere are stark warnings that speeders will lose their licenses. No one pays any attention, least of all to the threats against speeders.

Everybody cruises serenely 10 miles an hour over the posted limit, and the crank who doesn't becomes the object of intense motorist hostility. Out here in the dual-lane world, the man who stays on the speed limit is despised almost as deeply as the man who wants to make a left turn or pull into traffic from a roadside frozen custard stand.

The driver who has not been on the road all winter quickly remembers the old lesson that, out here, you have to move with the pack or be hated. At twilight, when the nerves can stand it no longer, there is the welcoming motel sign.

The motel is never really any place at all, whether the stationery proclaims it Melbourne, Fla., or Ellsworth, Me. This one, for example, lies next to a filling station and a neon sign about 40 feet high which says "Liquor."

A cellophane wrapper which says, "This glass has been sanitized for your protection" also says that the location is Delaware Township. The landmarks confirm nothing. Down the road is the universal American roadside restaurant in the universal American glass-and-plastic architecture serving the universal American plastic roadside meal.

The motel, which the children find so exciting, is unpleasantly suggestive, despite all its comforts, of some science-fiction nightmare. The "sanitized" drinking glass, the "message light" on the phone that will start flashing red if there is a message. The barely audible breathing of invisible heat ducts.

And, outside the curtained glass wall, the distant cries of swimmers from the pool, which is domed in corrugated plastic and heated to permit year-round bathing.

And, worst of all, the children feeding quarters to the massaging mattress. It is probably unrealistic to expect them to prefer a bed of pine needles, but it would be comforting to see some of the values of the old wilderness preserved. The pursuit of happiness ought to end some place more ennobling than "the land of tingling relaxation and ease."

GETTYSBURG

November, 1963—The chemistry of the American soil is sinister. Drench it in the blood of heroes and it brings forth a frozen custard stand.

Gettysburg is no exception. The battlefield nowadays is ringed in neon, wax museums, dioramas, cycloramas, the new instant motels, gimcrack dispensaries, two-bit battle flags, brass busts of Old Abe, tin bayonets and all the other paraphernalia of the Civil War tourist game.

The Wills House, where Lincoln touched up his speech for the cemetery dedication, has become a museum with two (not one, but two) life-size wax Lincolns. One grouping presents him with his wife and two of their children, none of whom appeared in Gettysburg. The other presents him alone in shirt sleeves in the bedroom, engrossed in the tragic blue funk commonly associated with the mythic Lincoln.

Poor Lincoln. The Civil War hagiographers deny him the right to humanity even in his bedroom. In the adjoining gift shop, one may buy a small plastic "camera" which, held to the eye and clicked, reveals Lincoln in portrait.

South of town, on Seminary Ridge, Robert E. Lee strides his metal charger (fine for climbing on the statue: up to $500) and gazes eternally toward the Bloody Angle at the Union center. In the mile of open ground between Lee and the Angle, the elite of Lee's army marched nobly to butchery and the Confederacy died and the Union was saved. In Lee's line of vision, beside Emmitsburg Road where Pickett's shattered line hurled itself up against the Federal cannon, the General now looks out on the inevitable custard stand.

All week long the tourist business has been brisk here, thanks to the concentration of politicians and pedagogues who have been praising and parsing the Gettysburg Address. Very little that is memorable seems to have been said.

The scholarly activity has centered on the quibbling over trivia that marks the true Civil War buff. How many speech drafts did Lincoln write? Which one did he deliver? How was the flag flown when he spoke? For the ceremonial reading Justice Michael Musmanno of the State Supreme Court, to whom the chore fell, surrendered to the electronic age by reading the speech to a tape recorder and having the canned version broadcast over the cemetery's public-address system.

The troubling question of Gettysburg, however, is whether the order that was imposed here in blood was moral or political, and few of the celebrants seemed as certain of the answer as Lincoln had been a century ago.

The battlefield itself answers no questions. At dusk in the plum sunsets of these raw November evenings it is studded with grotesque marble monuments and metal silhouettes of old generals. The field where Pickett's line came is terrifying . . . a mile of open ground ideal for butchery. What kept them coming? Surely not dedication to states' rights or slavery or hatred for the philosophic concept of union.

The only answers from the battlefield are those that explain every battle of every war: courage, discipline, foolhardiness, fear, resignation and conviction that somebody somewhere had a persuasive reason for requiring their deaths.

Lincoln did and managed to articulate it. The Confederacy was less fortunate in its leaders, who could never agree on what the great cause really was. "It's all my fault," Lee said here when he saw his army shattered. But was it? And what had he lost?

The politicians still can't decide, and the Civil War centennial goes on feeding us on a thin gruel of romance and frozen custard.

WEST VIRGINIA

The road to West Virginia slopes up from the seaboard through the moneyed green pastures of the Virginia hunt country, through Middleburg where the rich Yankee émigrés ride to hounds, past Atoka where the billboards advertise "Polo Every Sunday."

This is the American landscape as it should be. We instinctively recognize it from our daydreams and a hundred back issues of *Holiday* magazine. Emerald meadows and white board fences.

The morning air is sweet with the wafting perfume of folding money. The telephone lines hum with the voices of squires talking to their brokers and of consequential men checking up on Washington.

And then, as the road climbs another mountain, something

odd happens very abruptly. Virginia is suddenly gone. The road loops insanely toward a bottomless valley, and the melancholy of the Appalachians descends in layers.

Here the landscape is no longer curried and combed, but beautiful in a savage way, except where people have laid hands on it, and in these places it is scarred and sad. Jagged wounds disfigure it where miners have stripped the mountains' skin away to get at the coal, and gray wastes are piled by the creek beds.

The houses are no longer graceful, but merely serviceable. The people are no longer picturesque, but just rather poorly dressed. And out of the air, the radio picks the lugubrious chant of the rockabilly singer and the churchmen urging West Virginia to send money to relieve the poverty of Hong Kong.

West Virginians are tired of being told how poor they are. Ever since President Kennedy's 1960 campaign here jolted the American conscience, people have been traveling up from the fat rich seaboard to cluck over dying towns and undernourished children and defeated men, and West Virginians have developed the sensitivity of a poor relation who has had too much Sunday morning solicitude from rich cousins.

One response has been an impulse to put the artifacts of poverty out of sight and accentuate the positive. In Kanawha County, for example, a campaign is under way to tear down more than 500 abandoned shacks that mar the countryside.

Governor Barron is positively ebullient and can reel off figures to prove that 1962 was the best year economically in West Virginia history, that unemployment is down more than 50 per cent under his administration and that new industry is finally arriving to free the mountains from the smothering embrace of coal.

The official message from the Governor's office here is that "the outlook for West Virginia has never been better than it is right now." Perhaps this is true. It is difficult to argue with statistics, but there are still 50,000 people out of work here, and most of them are useless to the present American economy.

Others are working for six dollars a day in hazardous nonunion mining operations, digging coal from mines that have been abandoned because they couldn't be worked profitably at union wages.

But the most obvious testimony about West Virginia lies along the main roads between the Virginia hunt country and prospering Charleston. All the evidence of the great American boom is missing.

There are no new housing subdivisions in the towns, no new shopping centers or supermarkets, no new glass façades, no new schools, none of the monstrous new farming machines, no glittering glass motels.

At Charleston in the west, all this begins again, but Charleston is on the fringe. In the central counties, with the out-of-date towns and the out-of-date buildings and the people wearing out-of-date clothes, it becomes apparent that the future has leapfrogged the Appalachians.

In places like Clarksburg and Grafton, the American from megalopolis has the uneasy sensation of being displaced in time. They stir old memories of depression towns in the 1930's.

It nags at the mind, and the mountain air is heavy with the sense of a fundamental American failure.

DECATUR, ILL.

The awkward truth about automobile tourism in the United States will have to be faced if the Government hopes to lure the European multitudes here with cameras and coin.

At present, everything is overdone. Take the corn situation here in the Middle West. A European motoring westward up the Ohio River runs into the great August corn crop somewhere around Cincinnati. It is a magnificent spectacle, this thick green blanket matted so tightly that sunlight can barely penetrate to the stalks. It is one of the wonders of the world.

The traveler at first is awed by its grandeur. It rolls away to the horizon in green waves higher than a man can stretch. As the wheels move westward into Indiana, it becomes taller and thicker and richer, and the tourist marvels and feels humbled.

After an hour or two of cruising through deep corn, however, the spectacle begins to pall. One feels that his trip has had a sufficiency of corn. The car seat begins to feel hard and uncomfortable. A glaze begins to envelop the brain.

Somewhere in western Indiana, the motorist is seized by an overpowering need to get away from corn. The speedometer needle edges recklessly toward 75. The towering walls enclosing the two-lane road become a green blur stretching toward infinity. The driver begins to despise his traveling companions in their corn-drugged slumbers.

At the Illinois border, a genuine hatred for corn sets in. For hours and hundreds of miles, the traveler has been imprisoned in corn, and what Middle Westerners proudly call "the real corn country" has hardly begun. Ahead lie Illinois and Iowa, buried under an ocean of corn.

All along the way the radio chatters about newer and better fertilizers that will produce even more corn next year. The traveler shudders at the prospect, as the Agriculture Department must too, and if the traveler is a European he probably vows to warn his compatriots to go to Spain.

There is practically no relief from corn in the Middle West any more, short of fleeing into Chicago or St. Louis. There is an occasional small town like Danville, Ind., full of gentle people with uncorrupted faces, but the countryside has been dehumanized by the agricultural revolution. The farmer at work in the field is such a rare sight that travelers in the car wake up to stare, much as they do for a gas station or a turnpike.

The bounty all seems to be produced by grotesque machines and chemicals. There is very little need here for awkward inefficient man, who made a botch of it and had to be forced off the land. What is left is this incredible glut of wealth and an unutterable sense of loneliness, as the farms expand and fatten and the farmers disappear.

This is the visible aspect of the dusty statistics about the nation's move to the city. In thirty years, the farm population has dropped from 25 per cent of the national total to only 8 per cent. Here in Illinois total farm acreage has not declined significantly for twenty years, yet the number of farms has dropped by more than 25 per cent.

The Corn Belt would probably be difficult for the tourist in any case. If an equivalent piece of Europe—say, from Paris to Warsaw—were covered with corn, there would be fewer tourist dollars crossing the Atlantic. But the farm revolution that is killing the towns, removing the old farmhouses and silos from the landscape, and eliminating the farmer has tainted the natural beauty of the land with loneliness and monotony.

The occasional road worker along the way is greeted like a long-lost friend. And when one enters a town like Decatur, where someone has smeared paint on the billboard calling for the impeachment of Earl Warren, the heart leaps up to be back once again among disputatious human beings.

HANNIBAL, MO.

All over the world, wherever men can read, everyone knows Hannibal. Everyone has lived here for a precious moment, and there are few men who do not revisit it still in search of forgotten tranquility and lost dreams.

This Hannibal that belongs to the world exists only in a region of the mind. It is a place like Camelot and Troy, full of humanity at its best, better than life, yet, paradoxically, truer than life. Mark Twain, who spent his early years in the real Hannibal, created this paradise when he looked back from the saddened perspective of middle age and miraculously distilled the glory of boyhood in Tom Sawyer and Huckleberry Finn.

The real Hannibal, of course, was never much of a town, and it still isn't. Yet the power of Twain's magic is such that 175,000 persons come here each year to troop through the Mark Twain Museum and to stare at the reconstructed board fence which Tom set out to whitewash one warm Saturday morning just right for swimming.

The local paper keeps track of the visitors each day who have come the greatest distance. It is not uncommon to find a man from Australia. But whatever the tourist's point of origin, he must come expecting a letdown, knowing that it is bad policy to match real towns against towns that live in the imagination.

The pleasant surprise about Hannibal today is that it is still not a total disappointment. The road in from Illinois crosses the Mississippi on the Mark Twain Bridge, loops along Mark Twain Avenue past the Tom Sawyer Café, the Mark Twain Art Mart and the Tom and Huck Motel, then curves back to the river past billboards advertising the Mark Twain Cave, the Mark Twain Museum and the Mark Twain Boyhood Home.

The town's main shopping street is conventional Midwestern treeless. A ragtag row of gas stations and drowsing shops. "I can picture the white town drowsing in the sunshine of a summer's morning; the streets empty or pretty nearly so; one or two clerks sitting in front of the Water Street stores, with their splint-bottom chairs tilted back against the walls, a sow and a litter of pigs loafing along the sidewalk," Twain once wrote of it. And if allowances are made for the twentieth century, it is still much the same.

Across the street from Twain's home is the grander white frame house of Becky Thatcher, and in the Becky Thatcher Book Shop the sign says "Goldwater in '64." It seems perfectly right. After Tom and Huck came into that "awful sight of money"—$6,000 in robbers' gold—it was Becky's father, Judge Thatcher, who taught them the beauty of capitalism.

As Huck recounted it, "Judge Thatcher he took it and put it out at interest, and it fetched us a dollar a day apiece all year round—more than a body could tell what to do with." The Judge hasn't walked these streets for a century and more, but inside his house we can still feel the prudent ghost of an early Goldwater man, fretting about deficit spending and property rights.

The river is still alive with traffic, but the steam packets, whose daily arrivals once brought the town momentarily to life, are gone. Instead, there is a towering old stern-wheeler, the *River Queen,* now permanently moored at the Mark Twain Bridge, selling guided tours and shabby souvenirs.

In the evening the tourists sit in the faded plush grandeur of the dining saloon, eat catfish and study the fading movie posters which prove that Clark Gable once strode these very decks in planter's costume. Curtains of mayflies cling outside the windows, and the diners peer across the river and strain their imaginations to see rafts in the current and Jezebels at the bar.

In town there are still characters that Twain might have relished. Beside Tom's house is the museum of "Shoeless Joe from Hannibal, Mo.," a gentleman who clomps around in wooden clogs and kimono charging 10 cents admission to see relics of his army career.

And on the opposite corner, there is the short order cook at Bennett's Old Barber Shop Café, who has lived his life here and thinks it hilarious that anyone should come. "This may sound funny," he says, jerking his thumb toward the Twain home, "but all this seems like a junk pile to me."

There is no point in telling him about Troy and Camelot. He isn't the sort to grasp it.

COCOA BEACH

May, 1963—Life is strange here in the world of tomorrow, and the uninitiated visitor must expect to feel alien, lonely and baffled when he first arrives.

The men go barelegged and the women wear long pants.

Everybody wears sunglasses, sleeps in mechanically chilled air and talks in the new galactic slang.

Earnest bronzed men are forever saying things like "Gordo is in a very up condition" and announcing that they have just put a plastic liner in the sustainer turbo-pump. Weather forecasters sit around mumbling that they have three-quarters of the earth "under surveillance."

Up the road at Cape Canaveral, the world of tomorrow becomes a futuristic landscape of radar dishes and gantry cranes bursting out of a primitive waste of sand and palmetto where the armadillo and the rattlesnake still survive.

The billions that the Government is force-feeding into the space program burst out of the Florida sand in gaunt extrusions of steel and concrete, and people are pouring into Brevard County to get at the moon payroll.

Approaching Canaveral by highway from the north, a motorist notices the changes in the tenor of the billboards just below Daytona Beach. Back there they are still absorbed in the America of the present—internal combustion engines at the race track, tourist homes, Whataburger stands.

But as the road heads, flat and fast, for Canaveral, signs testify to a border crossing. Edgewater, 35 miles north of Cocoa, proclaims itself "Gateway to the Moon." Further on, Oak Hill, not to be outdone, introduces itself as "Gateway to the Universe."

At Cocoa there remain only vestigial traces of the tourist Florida, although on Cocoa Beach the motels are happy enough to entertain gawkers when there is no heavy rocket business afoot. Here, everything is earnest, urgent and ready for orbit.

This is a new Florida, and the big concentration of technicians may very possibly represent the truly new breed of American.

All this comes as a disappointment at first. The romance propagated about Cape Canaveral is misleading. The traveler comes as a pilgrim to see the poetry of man reaching for the stars; he finds instead a motel society built on cement blocks and nuts-and-bolts ideas.

Bureaucrats, technicians, mimeograph machine specialists,

public relations men, motherly creatures in fishnet hose running the beer at the motel lounges, blond bombshells at dawn on the Cape's beaches—these are the people who impose personality on the world of tomorrow.

Very quickly, of course, the pilgrim becomes a vital realist. After his first twenty-four hours, he listens without outrage while a young engineer from Texas explains that "consumables" have been added to Cooper's capsule.

He knows it would be a serious mistake to ask what "consumables" are. It would produce a ten-minute lecture of staggering technicality. Helpful girls would appear with bales of old mimeographed press releases about "consumables."

He begins, at night, to look back upon his day as a time when he was "no go" on a morning shave, pecan pie at lunch and an afternoon swim, but "go" on beer with dinner and a trip to the motel gift shop.

By this time, he is no longer appalled when his beer is brought by the motherly creature in fishnet hose. He may even find himself striking up absurd conversations with engineers from Texas, to demonstrate a proper spirit.

"That electron flux measuring device in the capsule—does it have a pocket ion chamber?" Or, "In what orbit will the xenon light cease to be visible to the astronaut?"

They all reach this stage. When they do, they're solid citizens of the world of tomorrow.

* * * *

The language that all the space people talk down here is called Spacespeak. It sounds like English, but it isn't.

In Spacespeak, people are constantly saying "all systems are Go." This means "the rocket is working O.K." No real Spacespeaker would be caught dead saying "O.K." "Mercury Control," which is Spacespeak for a gentleman named Shorty Powers, will occasionally say "A-O.K.," but purists consider even this a corruption.

"Go" is the word, and one of the toughest parts of a spaceman's job is "making Go, no-Go decisions." When unable to reach a "Go, no-Go decision," the spaceman is said to be "T minus and holding."

Acquiring fluency in Spacespeak is extremely difficult. Linguists rank it third, after Basque and Navajo, among the world's most obscure languages. Still, it is possible to learn a pidgin Spacespeak with relatively little study.

This won't be enough to get anybody past the sentries at Hangar S, but it will please the space people, who tend to look upon incorrigible English speakers with suspicion.

For example, nothing will brand a visitor here as un-space more surely than calling a "launch vehicle" a "rocket." This is the most abject confession of space ignorance; it is in a class with asking an admiral about his "boat." Calling the "launch vehicle" a "missile" would be almost as bad.

Spacespeakers use their "missiles" for war and their "launch vehicles" to put men and satellites into orbit. They never actually put anything into orbit, of course. They always "achieve orbital insertion."

If orbital insertion is not achieved, it is not because something goes wrong, but because of a "malfunction." Almost certainly, the "malfunction" will occur in a "system." "Systems" play a big part in Spacespeak.

There are many kinds of systems, but the most common are "the guidance system," "all on-board systems," "all systems" and "the most complicated system in the spacecraft," which is medical Spacespeak, meaning the astronaut.

As one master of Spacespeak confides, "Anything that goes wrong and you can't explain, you can always hang on the guidance system."

Technically, the machine that enabled Gordon Cooper to achieve orbital insertion was "a launch vehicle using the booster from the Atlas missile system." This, however, is getting pretty complicated, and the English speaker should not try it until he is comfortable in the basics.

Two words that must never be used are "yes" and "no." Say "affirmative" or "negative," and say it with authority. Cleverness with prepositions is also important, for they are welded indiscriminately onto all sorts of other words.

Space people, for example, would never dream of flying over Communist China; they "overfly" it, and then come back to talk about their "overflights." Their spacecraft do not splash into the water; they experience "splashdown."

"Splashdown," incidentally, is an exception to the rule that prepositions go on the front of Spacespeak words. ("Overflight," "onboard," "downrange," etc.) So is "countdown." By the rules, after declaring "all systems in a Go condition," they should proceed with the "downcount," but the approved word is "countdown."

If there is anyone not perfectly clear about all this, he might consider writing his Congressman on behalf of us all, and asking why the man we put on the moon cannot be trained to tell us plainly whether it is made of green cheese.

* * * *

Eventually the rockets will arrive and depart with timetable regularity.

A new generation of home owners will curse the noise and sue. Clocks will be set by the coming and going of the Mars Express. Small boys will be bored silly by old codgers rummaging through faded memories.

"You won't believe this, boy, but I can remember when the whole world used to come here and hold its breath, back when the first man went into space—"

Right now the rockets are risky vessels which run on uncertain schedules and produce strange emotions in the crowds that come to watch them. When there is a man aboard, as there was the other day when Gordon Cooper started his twenty-two orbits, the atmosphere is faintly suggestive of an Aztec sacrifice.

The eve is celebrated in revelry. Dawn find the traffic bumper to bumper for miles leading into Cape Canaveral. By 7 A.M. the sun is a furious blast of white heat in an iron sky.

Inside, the Cape is planet-by-Disney. Miles of bone-white sand and scrub. Here and there, dish-eyed radar on windowless blockhouses peer into your soul. At the press site, an old American ritual is in progress; a movie is being shot.

"All right," an authoritative voice bawls, "everybody look over toward the launch site." The press site is an artificially created mound carpeted in beautiful golf-greens sod. The mound is enclosed by a circular gray fence. Bleachers to the rear.

It suggests a dog show enclosure. Amplifiers boom the countdown news. An electrified world map shows the route proposed for Cooper. TV sets stand in the sunlight, camera batteries, telephones.

"Now, everybody look toward the launch site again," the movie producer commands. He is producing a film for N.A.S.A. It will illustrate the splendor of the press facilities. Cooper's rocket is a delicate silver tower silhouetted two miles across the scrub.

Cooper lies strapped on his couch waiting. Everyone is aware of the sacrificial role he must play if things go badly, but the thought remains unspoken. The reporters kill the minutes in gossip and admire the strange ladies who have turned up in the enclosure with press badges.

One affects the costume of early Hollywood, all crepe and elbow-length gloves. Another wears yellow toreador pants, gold Aladdin shoes, yellow sport shirt, yellow sport hair.

The air is full of small talk. Television voices keep saying "tension is mounting." The amplifier smothers the drama in trivia. "Tension is mounting," says a radio voice. "Essentially all the redundancy has been dropped," a man on television is explaining.

When the amplifier announces only five minutes until launch, conversations run down. People move quietly to the bleachers. The clock ticks through a great quiet, and for the first time you stare at the silver tower and give yourself up to thinking about the man on his couch, with all that fire and thunder about to explode beneath him.

The final seconds are counted away. The rocket erupts, rises trembling on a pillar of fire. The Hollywood lady clutches a handkerchief to her mouth. Standing, her whole body shudders as the Atlas rises, gathering speed and power.

A shock of sound roars across the sand. It is the infuriated snarl of a thousand express trains coming at you with open throttles. Television has never captured it, nor the blinding intensity of the rocket fire.

In two minutes it is over and out of sight. The amplifier is droning out vital statistics, and humdrum quickly returns. We are already becoming temperamentally prepared for the day when the rockets will arrive and depart with timetable regularity.

But for ten minutes or so, most of us can still feel the adventure of what is happening here, and when we become old codgers we will bore small boys silly recounting it.

WHITE SPRINGS, FLA.

The big stream in this part of the world is the Suwanee River, and the big Yankee, naturally, is Stephen Foster.

There is a Stephen Foster Colonial Inn, a Stephen Foster Museum full of Stephen Foster memorabilia, a gift shoppe full of Stephen Foster picture postcards, and a Stephen Foster carillon that plays Stephen Foster melodies. For some reason, there is not yet a Fosterburger stand nor a big Steveorama Used Car Company, but time will take care of this.

The carillon, the museum and a handsome piney park where the Suwanee flows are Florida's official homage to Foster in gratitude for his "Old Folks at Home," which is the state anthem. It is all done with the same grandeur that David O. Selznick lavished on "Gone With the Wind," and it has the same pleasantly narcotic effect on the beholder.

There are ironies, of course. Foster was a Pittsburgh man who knew little or nothing of the ante-bellum South he romanticized. He died destitute in Bellevue Hospital in New York.

Later, his brother, Morrison, wrote that the Suwanee had been selected for musical fame by purest chance. Stephen came to his Pittsburgh office one day to ask the name of a Southern river with two syllables that would fit a new song. Morrison first suggested the Yazoo, then the Pedee. Eventually, they picked Suwanee out of an atlas and Stephen shortened it to "Swanee."

For our own time, there are more pertinent ironies. The destitute Yankee balladeer who died a year before Lincoln is now trapped in the race quarrel. Here, in the museum the state has built to his memory, he seems firmly enlisted in the Confederacy.

A series of intricately detailed dioramas built to illustrate his songs depicts an ante-bellum dream world of happy pickaninnies and banjo strummers. "Old Black Joe," for example, finds Old Joe, nattily tailored in a brown tailcoat, leaning on a gnarled cane.

In the fields before him, happy slaves have happily at the cotton. A stern-wheeler plows the distant river. The colonnaded porch of Ole Massa's mansion is visible across the field, with a magnificent horse-drawn carriage awaiting Ole Massa's pleasure.

The "Swanee River" diorama is in the same spirit. Happy pickaninnies under the persimmon tree. Happy Uncle Tom talking happily to happy Aunt Jemima. The sternwheeler in the river with Gaylord Ravenal escorting an exquisite golden girl on deck.

This is the old South of fond remembrance among those who still insist that the Southerner "understands" the Negro, that the Negro would be happy here if "outsiders" would leave him alone. And, of course, it is the conceit so roundly despised by the new Negro.

This explains why Foster's songs are sung so rarely nowadays on radio, on television and in the schools. There is too much "Old Black Joe" in them, too much "Oh, darkies, how my heart is yearning!" They evoke a beautiful romantic America which, the Negro says, was always a lie.

If the Negro would like the romance debunked, there are many whites who would like to persuade themselves that the romance was pure. The Stephen Foster Museum comes down solidly on the side of romance, with its contented banjo strummers, its rosewood melodeon and dulcimer, and its lush oil portrait of Foster as a dreamy-eyed Ashley Wilkes surrounded by ladies swooning in magnolia blossoms. It is a strange end for a broken-down Yankee song writer who learned about Dixie in an atlas. And eventually, of course, there will be Fosterburgers to complete his canonization.

SYLACAUGA, ALA.

The roads of Dixie are mysterious women full of dark secrets and melancholy. They are fond of buzzards, scent themselves in honeysuckle and, like theatrical old bawds, slink about on swampy cushions trailing boas of Spanish moss.

They have little in common with Yankee roads. Yankee roads are great bores. They are always reminding you of how many people they have killed recently and boasting about their contributions to the Gross National Product. At heart, they are insurance salesmen.

The roads of Dixie, by contrast, despise salesmanship. An occasional billboard may point the way to a "washeteria" and the roof of a roadside pigpen may urge the snuff habit, but commerce clearly is not uppermost in their minds. Instead of boasts about the Gross National Product, they present a constant flashpast of American poverty at its most squalid.

Take Florida Route 100 west from U.S. 1. It heads out of Yankee Florida just above Daytona Beach and angles up through the wool-hat country toward south Georgia and Alabama. U.S. 1 is a Yankee road siphoning the pallid into the expensive sunshine of the Gold Coast. It is justly famous as a great road bore and is forever shouting nonsense like "See Living Wonders," "Smile and You Sell Friendly Florida" or "Don't Miss Manny's Alligator Center."

Route 100 introduces a new society of roads, carrying the motorist into a sullen loneliness of slash pine. For miles, though the road is good, there is no traffic in either direction. The heat closes in. The silence becomes a menacing substance.

Abruptly, the road introduces a display of towns where great oaks vault the streets and Spanish moss dangles from wires and men sit on store porches sweating and waiting for the universe to run down.

Conversation is possible. "Think it's gonna rain?" "Like I told a man come through here a little while ago, it's gonna rain when it comes to the end of this dry spell." Appreciative laughter.

In south Georgia the earth becomes red and the land becomes poorer. A haze of blue and pink wildflowers floats alongside the abandoned highway. The towns here are quiet ruins. The termites can be heard eating. The Negroes sit on collapsing porches of unpainted hovels.

A white hitchhiker from Albany, Ga., reports that the older Negroes are happy. "The older ones know how to be humble," he reports, "but these young ones are impudent." What makes the young Negroes impudent? "Agitators." It is the universal explanation heard everywhere. In every conversation the man without the regional accent feels the locals probing to discover if he is one of these wretched agitators.

Housing reaches bottom in southeastern Alabama along the rural highway beyond Phenix City. Here, much of the Negro housing would not meet the standards for housing hogs in northern Virginia. Unpainted hovels of one, sometimes two rooms. An ancient washing machine on the grass outside. Inside, silhouettes sitting on the floor.

The car radio is alive with church services and religious dramas. A minister cautions women against low-cut dresses, lipstick and short hair. Another urges his audience to "bathe in the word of God." In a typical playlet, a wife is held responsible for her husband's alcoholism because she "deliberately made Sunday a day for late sleeping and lazy breakfasts."

Occasionally, there is also "Big Johnny Reb," reading radio editorials in a doomsday baritone. Today, he is suggesting that the agitators disturbed the happiness of Birmingham to comfort Communists.

The roads of Dixie are too intoxicating to be taken in big doses. They quickly induce a dreamlike state in which the traveler becomes convinced that he is himself a dangerous agitator. He becomes fearful of conversation. It might betray his secret. He affects a bogus corn-pone accent. He buys a straw hat and galluses. The only antidote is to give up the roads of Dixie and go back to the Yankee roads.

THE COUNTRY DOES NOT EXIST

Returning to Washington after a few weeks out in The Country is an unnerving experience.

Brilliant young administrators are getting old, the elms are dying and people are standing around Federal antechambers reminiscing about the Eisenhower years. Suddenly, the Georgetown Volkswagens seem staid and middle-aged. They are full of frowns and worry lines, as if they expect soon to be traded in on new Cadillacs.

The worst thing is the cross-examination about the mood of The Country. The man who has been out in The Country knows there will always be absurd questions when he gets back, but at this pass in history they seem uniquely unanswerable.

"What is the thinking about Johnson now out in The Country?" "Is The Country ready for Goldwater?" "What does The Country think of tax reform?" "Is The Country disturbed about Congress?" The sensible thing would be to laugh the questions away, but it would also be cruel.

Here, in this humid tangle of politicians, such questions are taken very seriously. The locals can discuss them for days, for weeks. They are fascinated with the physical, mental, moral and spiritual conditions of The Country. A good earnest conversation about the mood of The Country is widely preferred to a lovely woman and moonlight.

What is equally strange is the general conviction that there really is a wonderful place called The Country. It is something like the land of Oz, a place full of juvenile excitements just beyond the rainbow, but unattainable to the adventurer who goes looking for it.

When the Washingtonian goes out past Bethesda or Leesburg, he discovers himself in a land of baffling variety, but back in the capital he is inevitably seized again by the devout conviction that, somewhere out there in all that teeming confusion, The Country exists.

It is a wonderful place that holds all the answers needed to edify the rulers. The problem is merely to get explorers there. On arrival, they have only to examine a few philosophical codgers, poll a scientifically selected sample of the natives, and solicit wisdom from cab drivers.

Then Washington will know what The Country is thinking about Johnson and whether The Country is ready for Goldwater. The trouble, of course, is that the explorers are always getting confused out there. And no wonder.

When you get out there, you discover that the people hardly ever think about De Gaulle or tax reform or Johnson. Instead, they are always asking how you liked your steak, when you plan to check out of your hotel, and whether you saw any rain in the neighboring county.

If they volunteer reflections on government, it is usually to denounce the local sewer commission. It is a safe bet that every voter in America votes against the local sewer commission in every election. But ask about politics and you get opinions phrased with Oriental cunning to deceive.

They tell you what they think you want to hear out there, or they tell you to mind your own business. Only an idiot would ask one of them, "Are you ready for Goldwater?" or "What is your mood?"

Out there in The Country the unpleasant truth becomes all too evident; The Country, as Washington imagines it, does not exist. There is only infinite variety; the moods are phantom; the wisdom of cab drivers is a malice toward lady motorists.

It would never do to come back to Washington and tell it like this. Such people are dismissed as incompetent, eccentric or impious. Senators, clairvoyants and the Attorney General have little time for them.

These people must know the mood of The Country. Then they will know whether to launch a crash program against the Dutch Elm disease and whether to switch Georgetown from Volkswagens to Cadillacs. Who dares tell them that The Country is just a dream?

PART 6

THE NATION'S CAPITAL, AND MORE'S THE PITY

NO, THE COUNTRY DOES NOT EXIST

"In accordance with Article 3 of the bylaws of the Brotherhood of Washington Correspondents, this panel is convened to hear charges that you, the accused, did bring obloquy and ridicule upon the Brotherhood and did negligently and recklessly expose it to the most severe prestige damage, as a result of the reporting done by you, the accused, during the course of a 2,500-mile trip through the United States of America, hereafter specified as 'The Country.' How do you plead?"

"I tried, but it was terrible out there—"

"The accused is not in order. No emotional displays will be tolerated in the chamber. Pull yourself together, man. We all know what it's like to go into 'The Country.' "

"You can't tell what's going on out there. I tried, I went all the way out the Ohio Valley, down the Mississippi, across Tennessee and up through the Cumberlands. I tried to find the mood of 'The Country.' I tried to learn what 'The Country' was thinking. Everywhere I stopped, I looked for ugly significance, disturbing trends, ominous developments that would shake the foundations of NATO—"

"This panel has studied your reports and found only the most miserable assortment of trivia. Here, for example, you say, 'In the Midwest one is far more conscious of corn than of Lyndon Johnson.' How do you think it makes your colleagues feel to see that sort of piffle in print?"

"But it's the truth."

"That's no defense. We are all sitting here in Washington writing that 'The Country' is on fire about Lyndon Johnson, and you are out there reporting on corn. What about the insiders, eh? Did you look up the insiders and ask them what 'The Country' felt about Lyndon Johnson?"

"I wanted to talk to some insiders, but I couldn't recognize them when I got out there. Everybody there looks like outsiders."

"A craven admission of incompetence. What about taxi drivers? Didn't they tell you anything?"

"Taxi drivers never say anything to me that's very interesting."

"What about the typical Missouri farmer? Any correspondent who goes into 'The Country' and doesn't talk to the typical Missouri farmer—Well, it's incredible."

"I looked for the typical Missouri farmer all the way from Hannibal to St. Louis, but everybody said he was sailing the Isles of Greece with his family."

"Look at these notes. Not a single interview with powerful Midwestern Republican circles. Not a quotation from worried mothers. Here's an entry that says: 'Sign on barn outside Clarksburg, W. Va.—Relax and enjoy it.' What does that mean?"

"I thought I might write something about American barn signs."

"I see. Get the insiders to tell you what all the barn signs mean for the Administration's tax program, I suppose? Not a bad idea. But what's all this gibberish? I read the following page from accused's notebook into the record: 'Rock City is beautiful beyond belief.' 'Babylonianism.' 'Take a kid fishing in Tennessee.' 'Don't let lifted eyes in Hell be yours.' 'Prince of Peace and our soon coming Lord.' "

"Well, I was in Tennessee, you see, and I had the feeling that I wasn't getting the mood of it, and I couldn't find any insiders anywhere to fill me in on the South's attitude toward Goldwater. So I saw this bumper sticker that said, 'Goldwater for President; Johnson for King,' and I thought, if I could jot down all the bumper stickers and billboard slogans I saw, I would get an interesting reading on the mood of

Tennessee. When I collected them all, it was obvious that Tennessee was much more interested in Hell and Salvation than in Goldwater, but I couldn't mix religion and politics."

At this point an incredulous silence fell upon the trial panel. Judgment and sentencing followed swiftly. As usual, the sentence was not made public, but the insiders say that the mood of the panel was ugly.

CITY OF MOONBEAMS

It is gray and windy here and at night there is an evil white moon which laughs at the F.B.I.

Recently a crew from the state projectile factory sent a camera to the moon to take pictures. The National Security Council was curious to know why the moon was laughing and whose side it was on in the struggle for men's minds. The camera never came back.

Men in ten-gallon hats and three-button suits are standing on marble steps throughout the city trying to reassure passers-by. They are certain to get to the bottom of this moon affair before 1970, they insist. The people, for the most part, hurry past them with eyes averted.

A short time ago, a man had his name taken down for arguing. "Why are you so sure we will win the race for space and therefore beat Communism in the struggle for men's minds?" the man asked. "Because we are able to put more sand into space than any other great power," came the reply. "Right now, for example, we are orbiting 50 per cent more sand than any other washday product."

"You talk like a soap salesman," said the skeptic. "My advice to all of you is, Leave that moon alone." Whereupon the man's name was taken down by the police and circulated among his neighbors, who, fortunately for him, reported that he kept regular hours, drank little and always spoke well of Chiang Kai-shek.

The big house of the Leader here is dark and eerie under the bone-white moonlight. The Leader treads through the big house at night snapping out lights. There are rumors that he is quite gone on the subject. He has been telling people he must hold down the light bill so there will be enough money left to go to the moon and win the struggle for men's minds.

The townspeople say that the Leader is entitled to a few idiosyncrasies, considering the problems he has. For one thing the Inspired Man from over the sea has been going around saying that the Generalissimo has no clothes on. This had been whispered around town for several years, but everybody had agreed not to say it aloud because of the general understanding that two or three Congressional committees were ready to ruin anyone who did.

The Leader may also be distracted by the vulpine barking of his enemies who hope to put him out of the big dark house. The townspeople dread these marauders, who fly through the air and alight without warning to deliver their fearful boring attack.

They come in many guises. Some stand on street corners showing their teeth. It is best to go around the block to avoid this kind. He seizes his victim by the hand, shows his teeth and says, "As I can display more teeth than any other borer, I am clearly the nicest fellow around and should therefore be made the Leader."

Others take the opposite tack, seizing the victim's hand and urging him to let his old mother pay her own hospital bills and saying, "I am clearly the meanest fellow around and should therefore be made the Leader." Others seize the townspeople by the ears and shout things like, "Since you insist that I sacrifice myself to become the Leader, my inner nobility constrains me to give in."

These borers rarely talk about anything that is uppermost in the minds of the townspeople. They are given to tedious explanations of why the Generalissimo really does have clothes on even though he looks naked and how the struggle for men's minds can be won by putting sand into orbit with more imagination. On more vital questions, they are intellectually limp.

Ask, "What will you do to restore my enthusiasm?" and they tell you about Social Security. Ask, "What will you do for peace of mind?" and they tell you about the struggle for men's minds. Ask, "Why is that evil moon laughing at the F.B.I.?" and they tell you that if they are elected they will wipe that smirk off the moon's face.

Tell them, "Let that moon alone," and they will signal for policemen to take your name.

COCKTAILS KENNEDY STYLE

The sound of the Washington cocktail party varies from year to year, from season to season. In January, 1963, it sounded like this:

"Isn't it thrilling just being in Washington these days? I mean, being able to tell your grandchildren that you were here at the same time as the Mona Lisa and all that! And just when the Ted Kennedys are moving into Georgetown too. . . ."

"Waiter, Waiter! . . . He just won't pay any attention to me, darling. . . ."

"Sorry, did you say the Ted Kennedys are moving the Mona Lisa to Georgetown? How chic! But won't the Italians hate it!"

"It wasn't the Italians, darling. It was the French who lent it to us. It was painted by the Italians. Oh, waiter!"

"I'll bet they've got a thousand people crammed into this place, and more coming every minute, too."

"Well, I went to see the Mona Lisa on the opening night, of course. The night the President was there, and everyone behaved so terribly. Well, I thought to myself, isn't this a travesty of culture? I'll bet Michelangelo is turning over in his grave."

"It wasn't Michelangelo, was it? It was Leonardo."

"Michelangelo. Leonardo. There are so many of them to keep straightened out. All I know is that they're all wonderful . . . yes, waiter, it's a daiquiri. . . ."

"Have I been to the ballet this week? Are you kidding? With my district, if I ever got caught at the ballet, I'd never get elected dog catcher again. Don't get me wrong: I like culture as well as the next guy, but ballet—You just don't know the American voter if you think they're ready for ballet in this country."

"Listen, let's get out of this mob. We can go to my place and turn the lights down and listen to the Ravel quartets. . . ."

"Harry, do we have to drink wine all the time when we go out? In this riot nobody would notice if we forgot the wine bit and had some bourbon. . . ."

"Good evening, Mister Secretary. Saw you at the Mona Lisa opening the other night."

"A masterpiece, isn't she?"

"Pure genius."

"One of mankind's culminating achievements."

"I always say, the mind of Socrates, the vision of Leonardo, the wisdom of Shakespeare, the divinity of Beethoven, the humanity of Tolstoy. These are the great monuments of our heritage."

"Well, of course, you have to remember there are giants in our own time, speaking culturewise. . . ."

"Waiter, has the scotch run out?"

"I mean, culturewise, men like Rusk and McNamara and Dillon may not go down as great creators, but they'll be remembered as appreciators. . . ."

"That's right. For the first time in its history, this town has appreciators to set the tone of its cultural posture. It's men like Rusk and McNamara who have helped Mrs. Kennedy lead this town out of the cultural swamps. I'll tell you, men like that simply wouldn't come to the White House to listen to Fred Waring. You've got to give them Sandburg, Shakespeare, bossa nova, Leonardo da Vinci, or they just wouldn't come to the White House, that's all. Waiter, do you think you could take this sherry glass and let me have that double martini . . . ?"

"Harry, what is a cultural posture?"

"Something like defense posture. That's Pentagon talk, but it doesn't mean anything exactly. . . ."

"Remember a few years ago, how we used to think American movies were fun? What a long way we've come to maturity. . . ."

"We've grown up, that's all. Hey! That woman over there in the green wig! Isn't that . . .?"

"Don't be silly. You don't think she would be caught dead at a blast like this?"

"Waiter, what do I have to do to get a scotch?"

"Oh, you can talk all you want to about Chekhov and Proust, but I say the really great cultural spirits have always been political. I mean, take Pericles. Take Franklin Roosevelt. They were men that made posture culturable. . . . I mean, made culture possible. Gosh, I forgot where I parked my Volkswagen."

"Waiter, waiter . . . a martini, je vous en prie . . . I mean, s'il vous plaît. . . ."

WASHINGTON'S FAVORITE SPORT

These manhunts that Washington loves so much are morbidly fascinating. The town knows that they are at best unsporting, like a bush-league bullfight, and at their worst, obscene, like a public hanging; but it cannot resist them.

The reasons for this are as hard to explain as the Englishman's joy in cricket. Cricket expresses the English temperament; manhunting fulfills the Washingtonian. Memorable manhunts become historical watersheds. "The time they got Alger Hiss" immediately suggests a whole era of American history. This occurred just before "the time they got Owen Lattimore."

Then came "the time when Joe McCarthy got the State Department," "the time they got Joe McCarthy," "the time they got Sherman Adams," and "the time they got Charles Van Doren." This year will doubtless be remembered as "the time they got Bobby Baker."

Opponents of manhunting are always objecting that the sport is cruel and unfair. Of course it is, but this explains only a small part of its peculiar fascination for this most peculiar town.

The typical manhunt begins with the wounding of the quarry. Politicians and newsmen rush out and plunge headlines into his quivering flanks. Trumpets proclaim him a violator of the conventional morality. The bullfight's opening knives merely weaken the beast for later killing, but the first blows of the manhunt usually destroy the quarry's reputation before the fun starts.

The town then settles back to watch him bleed and make book on whether he will go to prison. Misanthropes go about rejoicing in the renewed conviction that nobody is above mistrust, and town whispers inflate the victim's sins to loathsome proportion.

The charm of the really great manhunts lies in the strange emotional blend they produce in the spectator. From the bleachers, the hunted man becomes an object of both pity and contempt.

Invariably, he is a pillar of rectitude and respectablity—like Hiss, Lattimore, Van Doren or Adams—and from Washington bleachers it is perversely satisfying to see rectitude and respectability torn down. It sends the crowd home to cocktails happily confirmed in the sanctity of its own mediocrity.

If a victim like Owen Lattimore survives to prove that the whole hunt was a ghastly miscarriage of public morality, it doesn't really matter. Washington will say, as it still does of Lattimore, "If he hadn't been so smug with the committee we might not have ruined him quite so thoroughly."

In the average hunt, however, connoisseurs take keenest delight from noting how the quarry's commonplace human lapses are used to destroy him. When the Hiss hunt was on, for example, it seemed very sinister that Hiss could not remember housefurnishing details of a home he had lived in a decade earlier.

Most men, of course, can't remember how their wives had the parlor furniture arranged last summer and they know that a clever Senator could ruin them for such a memory lapse. The vicuña coat given Adams by his pushy friend, Goldfine, has its counterpart in the thousands of innocent gifts that change hands here every Christmas.

What man doesn't know that they are innocent? Yet, who would want to defend them in headlines?

Bobby Baker, it was charged, used his Senate clerical position to improve private income. This cannot be excused by the fact that Congressmen do the same thing, but the fact helps keep the affair in proper perspective. In its fury, however, the hunt was expanded into innuendo about Baker's private club where, it was whispered, the waitresses wore black net stockings.

This sounds ugly, but as every cleancut boy who has ever been to Cape Canaveral knows, the American obsession with black net stockings has reached a pitch where grandmothers have to wear them if they want work hustling beer. How many habitués of the Cape would want to answer headlines charging that they had had beer from grandmothers in black net hose?

And so the ultimate spectator appeal of the manhunt is a little clearer. Everyone in the bleachers who has lived as people do in the mid-twentieth century realizes that he is just as vulnerable as the man in the witness chair. Somebody has to pay. The man in the bleachers thanks his stars that the hounds have not chosen him.

WITNESS

In the Capitol's waiting room for key witnesses, two men find themselves alone, awaiting their turns to be called into committee chambers:

"You spend a lot of time here?"

"A lot of time. I've seen 'em come and I've seen 'em go. Chambers, Hiss, Elizabeth Bentley, Harvey Matusow, Frank Costello, Paul the Waiter. I've seen them all sitting right there where you're sitting now. Some went to jail and some named names and some got named before they could name names."

"What's it like in there?"

"When you go on the stand before the committee, you mean? Well, I don't think it'll be too bad for you, seeing as how you're a mystery witness."

"How did you know I was a mystery witness?"

"That black executioner's hood you're wearing, it's a dead give-away. They always put it on the mystery witnesses. Makes a good news photo. Wakes up the reporters. Gets the committee on television. I've worn it myself a few times. I don't know about you, but it always gives me a new feeling of power."

"Did it make you feel as though you might name more important names than you planned to before you put it on?"

"That's it! I wore it once before Internal Security and I named names so big that the committee had to get a new appropriation to give them all a chance to clear themselves. Not all of them made it."

"Funny, that's exactly the way I feel. I'm going to go in there and name names I wouldn't dream of naming if I didn't have this hood on, and tonight I'm really going to be scared."

"Don't let it start you to brooding. You're a key witness, aren't you? The committee is counting on you. If you start brooding, you'll go to pieces after two or three appearances and you'll be washed up as a key witness before you've had your first book published. Think about your future, man! What committee are you going before? Un-American Activities, Permanent Investigations, Internal Security?"

"None of those. It's the subcommittee investigating Administration news management."

"Good stuff, that. Something new and stimulating to the public. Just between us, I think the public's had it with the Communism bit for a while. . . ."

"Why are you whispering? Speak up."

"Shhh. This room may be bugged. Say something nasty about Khrushchev."

"Never mind that. I want to know how to live with myself when I get through naming these names."

"Well, what's your line? Were you a reporter who let your news be managed? Now you're contrite. You've seen the error of your ways. You know the evil that managed news can bring to the country. Conscience compels you to tell everything and ask the committee's mercy. In duty to your country, you must name colleagues and friends you have seen eating with George Reedy or speaking humanely of Arthur Sylvester at the Pentagon or. . . ."

"No, you've got it wrong, I'm afraid. I was on Government's side helping to manage the news."

"Then you will testify, I assume, to clandestine meetings in Georgetown houses where the mechanics of news management were explained by men high in Government. You will tell of acting as courier to relay these plans to news managers throughout Washington?"

"Something like that, I suppose. With this hood on, I can feel some really powerful testimony coming on."

"What an opportunity! The TV panels will be screaming for you. The mags will want pieces under your signature. Then, your book: "I Was a News Manager for Lyndon Johnson." Serialization. Hollywood. Ah, how I wish I had your future!"

"Why shouldn't I have fame? After all, these have been thankless years with Government. I'm entitled to something. I'll name some good names today, but not too many. They'll have to have me back, and I'll name some more good names."

"Name it up."

"When you think about it, news management really is an evil that could destroy democracy unless someone has the courage to speak out. . . ."

THE MISSILE GAP REVISITED

Chester Carrothers, the ill-informed man, was in Washington on one of his infrequent visits recently and, as usual, spent an afternoon browsing through the antiques of Americana stored in the Smithsonian Institution.

After admiring the cutlass collection and working the steam-engine models, he paused in dismay before an unusual display just off the main corridor. "What in the world is that remarkable exhibit?" he asked.

"Why, that's the missile gap." Carrothers seemed baffled. "Surely you knew that the missile gap had been given to the Smithsonian as a national treasure? They haven't mounted it very well, I'm afraid. There was some talk about suspending it from the ceiling, like the Spirit of St. Louis."

"Missile gap," said Carrothers. "Don't think I ever heard of it."

"The missile gap, sir, made history in this town for two or three years during the Eisenhower Administration. It was the proof positive that under Eisenhower the country had fallen behind the Soviets in missile development and would be so far behind during the 1960–64 period that the Russians would be able to push us all over the map."

Carrothers seemed unimpressed. "It doesn't look so scary," he said.

"That's because you see it here in its collapsed form. As we now know, the missile gap was not only infinitely expandable, but also collapsible. When the Democrats extended it to its full size, it was very impressive indeed. Here, let's open it up."

With a push of the button controlling the exhibit's wiring, the missile gap began to assume terrifying proportions. Carrothers gulped. "Stop it," he whispered.

"See what I mean? It shows unmistakably that the Russians have at least a five-year jump on us in the ability to drop nuclear warheads all over the globe. To get the full effect, however, you must hear the sound effects."

With the push of another button a blood-curdling cacophony of Democratic voices began reciting the perils of the missile gap. The voices of two Democratic Senators, Jackson of Washington and Symington of Missouri, were distinctly audible forecasting a siege of Soviet "nuclear blackmail."

"Hey," said Carrothers, "that's a familiar voice saying that the United States during the 1960–64 period will be in 'great peril' because of Soviet 'offensive and defensive missile capability.' Don't I know that voice?"

"That is John F. Kennedy speaking in 1958."

"But whose is that faint voice in the background saying that we have nothing to worry about?"

"That's Eisenhower, also 1958."

"Terrifying," said Carrothers. "Who built the contraption?" It was explained that some thought it had been built by the Democratic National Committee to scare the country into voting Democratic in 1960 and that some thought it had been built by Air Force Intelligence out of misinformation gathered about Russian missile activities.

"And all the time it was only a bogeyman," Carrothers said.

"Secretary of Defense McNamara said in the *Saturday Evening Post* that it was just a 'myth.' This country, he said, 'created a myth of its own weakness' and had to end the myth in order to make possible 'a firm line with our adversaries.' Now, you see, we actually have many more missiles than the Russians, which is why we were able to treat them so roughly in Cuba."

"What I can't understand," Carrothers said, "is why the Democrats don't build a monument to it if it really persuaded so many people that the Republicans were ruining the country."

"Come, now, Mr. Carrothers. You can't build a monument to a myth, to a thing that doesn't exist. Look here." The guide pushed a third button and a squad of men from Central Intelligence and the Democratic National Committee emerged from the woodwork, folded the missile gap into small pieces, dropped them into a trash can, then bowed to Carrothers. "There. You see? It's not only collapsible. It is also disposable."

FILIBUSTER

January, 1963—A typical afternoon in the filibustered Senate these days goes something like this:

Time: 1:45 P.M. Atmospheric conditions: somnolent. The dead air of the chamber has the stale morning smell of Pullman cars. The artificial light is a tired yellow, the type peddled by sharp used-sunlight dealers to gullible Architects of the Capitol.

The visitor has the eerie sensation of being sealed deep in impenetrable depths of stone, encased against time and circumstance. Surely, in this remote place nothing of importance to living man could ever have happened. Is there a hint of mummy dust on the red figured carpet?

In the galleries are 166 persons, including one group of

about seventy-five schoolchildren teetering on the brink of slumber. On the floor, four senators, including Lister Hill of Alabama, assigned to keep the filibuster going through the early afternoon.

Of the other three, only Spessard Holland of Florida listens. It is Holland's duty to revive Hill's spirits now and then by rising to ask him a question, like, "Isn't it true that any senator who indulged in unlimited debate on a matter on which he lacked sincere conviction would destroy the confidence of the public?"

To which Senator Hill can reply, "The senator is so correct, and I deeply appreciate his making this contribution."

What is the filibuster about? It seems that some senators want to make it harder to filibuster. This has provoked the Southern senators to filibuster against efforts to make it harder to filibuster. The point of the thing, however, seems very remote here in the heavy, ancient air. Nobody expects anything to come of it; it is a charade played out with tired desperation. Time: 1:47 P.M. Senator Hill is reading the famous history of the right of unlimited debate in the Senate. It is a familiar tale which every Southern senator knows by heart and recites at great length whenever called upon to filibuster. It is a tale that starts with George Washington and contains chapters for each of the heroes of American politics.

"And here's what Senator Henry Cabot Lodge said, and I quote . . ." Hill is saying. Lodge Sr., it appears, was on the Southern side. In the West Gallery a handsome brunette in black dress and sunglasses sleeps soundly.

Hill drones on, denouncing Vice President Charles G. Dawes for urging limitation on Senate debate in the Coolidge era. On the Republican side of the chamber, Kenneth B. Keating of New York unfolds in a cavernous yawn. ". . . I recall a great senator from the State of Wisconsin, Senator LaFollette," Hill is saying. In the Vice President's chair, presiding over the Senate, Senator Daniel Inouye browses in the Congressional Record.

"Isn't it true . . . ?" Senator Holland is asking Hill.

"So true . . . exactly," Hill agrees.

"Then, there must be imposed, must there not . . . ?" Holland asks.

"The senator is so correct, and I deeply appreciate his making this contribution," says Hill.

A scholarly looking youth sleeping in the West Gallery is shaken awake by the doorkeeper and chastised. This is no place for sleep. . . . "Rome lost her liberty and we know of her decline and fall," Senator Hill is saying.

Suddenly, a ripple of excitement stirs the galleries. On the floor, Senator J. Glenn Beall of Maryland is tugging at Hill's sleeve. He wants permission to interrupt. Hill agrees. Beall addresses the chair. The moment is tense.

"I rise," Beall declares, "to defend the name of the fair State of Maryland against an insult." Silent consternation in the chamber. "I resent the crab cakes being served in the Senate dining room today being called 'Maryland crab cakes.' " he declares, waving the menu.

"No Marylander would recognize what is being served patrons of our dining room," he says. "I want the world to know that those crab cakes are not Maryland crab cakes."

The excitement subsides. For a moment, the Senate has come perilously close to the problems of Twentieth Century life. "What is sorely needed in Congress," Hill continues, "is seldom greater speed. . . ."

"Is it not true," Holland asks, "that the Senate is more than an ordinary legislative body . . . ?"

The clock ticks. A boy in the gallery dozes. A passing senator yawns. Somewhere beyond the impenetrable stone, there is said to be life and movement. And in the Senate, Hill is saying, ". . . Mr. Jefferson declared. . . ." And Holland is asking, "Isn't it true . . . ?"

MOSS, ALL IS MOSS

For the first year or two after Congress had come to a full stop, no one could quite believe that it was really beyond repair.

Superficially, everything seemed to be running as normally as ever, and people who pointed out that damp rusty vapors were coming from the cellar were dismissed as Cassandras. Each day, just before the stroke of noon, Speaker John McCormack would appear, as he always had, smoking his beloved cigar, to announce that none of the President's bills could be enacted.

In the Senate, the familiar old routine seemed to be going on with clockwork regularity. Senator Morse continued to declare that vicious attacks by unprincipled enemies of the Republic would never deter him from the fight to save humanity. Senator Russell went on delivering, at periodic intervals, his famous defense of the filibuster.

In the caucus room, Senator McClellan's interrogations of rascals and gorillas continued to amuse national television audiences, as though nothing unusual had really happened. Month after month, as he always had, Chairman Mills declared that medical care for the aged was dead in committee, and Senator Harry F. Byrd went right on announcing that tax reform would have to wait until next year.

Finally, of course, it became impossible to pretend that everything was all right. In 1963, after Congress had sat in the Capitol for the whole year just listening to the hum of the air-conditioning, children began snickering and scandalous rumors began circulating.

By the late 1960's, after Congress had sat in continuous session for six years and produced only seven appropriations bills and two resolutions (deploring Communism and fire-ant depredation in the South), the Lampwick Commission delivered its historic report.

Those old enough to remember that period will recall the public's incredulous response when the commission reported that Congress had long since slipped through a keyhole in the time-space continuum and escaped from the human concept of time. In the typical Senate committee room, they found, years might pass while the committee performed the work of a single day.

When Chairman Mills talked of getting around to medical care for the aged "next year," they concluded, he was quite sincere. But "next year" in Congressional time, they demonstrated, would not come in earth time until the twenty-fifth century.

The discovery of the hideous coat of moss that had grown out of the machinery and was beginning to spread through the entire building precipitated the crisis. The President's proposal for a radical moss elimination program—the only request he made in that year's State of the Union message—was doomed from the start.

Speaker McCormack appeared, as he always had, smoking his beloved cigar, to announce that the moss bill could not be enacted. Senator Morse said that he would tie up the Senate for weeks rather than fatten the purse of the moss-killer trust. Senator Byrd said that he had 405 witnesses who wanted to testify in committee on the moss bill and that he couldn't see how he could finish hearings until next year.

The upshot, as every schoolboy knows, was the bitterly controversial Preservation Proclamation, under which Congress was made a branch of the Smithsonian Institution and the Agriculture Department was put in charge of a crash moss-eradication program.

As a result, this relic of the nation's heritage has been lovingly preserved in its original form. Today's visitor can come and watch these quaint figures behave just as they did in real life. Each day, just before noon, Speaker McCormack still appears, smoking his beloved cigar, to announce that none of the President's bills can be enacted.

On clockwork schedule, Senator Morse still denounces the unprincipled, Senator Byrd still says that taxes must wait until next year, and Chairman Mills still announces that it looks bad for medical care for the aged.

No one can visit it without marveling at the hardiness of these early Americans.

LIFE IN THE C.I.A.

News item: The Central Intelligence Agency recently broke its traditional policy of silence by holding a press conference to announce its findings on the state of the Soviet economy.

The break from tradition was in part an effort to improve C.I.A.'s image by publicizing its successes. In the past C.I.A. has complained that the public hears only of its failures—as in the U-2 case and at the Bay of Pigs—but does not appreciate the high quality of the bulk of its operations.

"Hello, Mr. McCone. This is Staggers here. How's everything in the spy game these days? . . . Staggers, sir. That's S-T-A-G. . . . That's right, sir. . . . With Hodding, Footling & Smelt. I'm the new man on the account and I have a couple of ideas here I'd like to run up the flagpole. . . . How's that, Mr. McCone? You don't like the slogan? . . .

"I thought it was kind of catchy. 'Spy American.' . . . I know it doesn't make much sense, but wait till you hear it to an orchestral background with that big trumpet sound. . . . Well, let's put it on the back burner for awhile, Mr. McCone. . . . Forget about it? . . . All right, Mr. McCone, you're the top spy. Listen, about the Bulgarian caper. . . .

"All right, sir, 'The unfortunate trial in Bulgaria.' I was wondering whether we haven't got a great story to tell there. You see, sir, the Commies are saying we paid this Bulgarian

200,000 bucks and a lot of people around here are complaining that a Senator has to work ten years for that kind of money. . . .

"You want to play down the 200,000? . . . Well, I realize it could drive prices up all over Eastern Europe, Mr. McCone, but you've still got that Bay of Pigs mess hanging over your image, remember. . . . All right, sir, have it your way, but don't forget the State Department is downgrading your work at every chance. . . . Now, about this fellow Bond you're sending to take care of that phony Communist pasha in Monte Carlo. He's right here with me now. . . .

"Yes, I know he's an amazing agent, sir. . . . Tremendous tolerance to pain, eh? . . . That's what I wanted to bring up, sir. From an image point of view, I think he's all wrong. . . . Too British. Too free with the girls. Too sharp with the cards. . . .

"Well, I thought it would be a good opportunity to send a camera team along and a couple of script writers and get something on film. You know, Bond on the beach with the pasha's girl friend, Bond bilking the pasha at baccarat. I think the networks might go for it, but frankly, Mr. McCone, I wouldn't recommend a British type for best image results. . . .

"Cameras are out? . . . Well, why don't I just send a writer and tell him to hoke it up a little bit—you know, make Bond a little more Nebraska. We could leak it to *The Saturday Evening Post* . . . right . . . right . . . right. . . . Oh, Mr. McCone! I see why they made you the top spy. . . . I'll tell him . . . Bond, the Chief says if you can get into British Secret Service headquarters and find out who's handling their public relations we'll get you a guest shot on 'I've Got a Secret.' . . .

"Uh—what do you want to know that for, Mr. McCone? . . . Oh . . . I see. . . . Well, we're doing our best. . . . The Bay of Pigs wasn't our fault, you know. . . . You didn't think much of the press-briefing idea on the Soviet economy either. . . .

Oh, you like it? . . . But you think we should have pulled it off without letting the press know it was an agency image-builder? . . . That's pretty harsh talk, Mr. McCone. . . .

Frankly, sir, if you'll excuse me, you can either run a taut spy shop or you can build yourself a fine public image, but you can't do both. . . . Mr. McCone, you'd never guess what Bond is doing now. . . .

"No. . . . Not that either. . . . He's driving bamboo slivers under his fingernails. . . . So help me. . . . And lighting them with matches. . . ."

THE ADDLE OF MEN'S MINDS

"It must be terribly exciting, sir, living here at the Center of the Political Maelstrom. Can you tell us what the candidates are talking about?"

"Ility, idity, ism and ment. Race, space, Cuba and faith. These are issues the nation must face. Year of hysteric decision."

"Is there some question, then, about this country's ility?"

"Reliability of surviveability capability and viability of Cuba culpability are heavily ized by Thegrandoldparty. Democrats claim flexibility of bangability, boomability and doomability, blame Grandoldparty's Cubidity for narrow escape from deterrence occurrence in 1962, and minimize Republican charges as fidel-faddle."

"What a thrilling clash of ideas! What remedies do the candidates propose?"

"Candidates urge more ship—statesmanship, leadership, followership. They pledge to accelerate the pace, step up the race, economize on space and maximize the faceability of the future, without regard to racecreedorcolor. They will implement the increment, crucialize the dignity of man and finalize peacism.

"But isn't the Bobby Baker affair an issue?" "Utilization of rascal irresponsibility charges is effectuated for maximum feasibility in fourteen-point foreign policy statements seizing the initiative with declarations to the effect that the peace race pace has been re-tardinized by Bakerism."

"If you will pardon a personal question, how long have you been talking like this?"

"Capability to project image of responsibility while magnitudinizing flexibility to minimize wit first noted after six months exposure to Center of Political Maelstrom. Vital weapon in the addle for men's minds—I mean, battle for poverty—poverty—poverty—poverty——."

"Your needle is stuck."

"It does that more and more lately. Where were we?"

"Which party is better equipped to prevent the ization of the world?"

"The party that can turn back Communism and bombunism and spread momunism among uncommitted peoples. The party that can most efficiently incorporate a posture of unwinceability abroad with a poorsture of plenty in Appalachia. The party that can expedite moonability, expend appropriations with decreasing impact on the taxpayer sector, expand the national dross product, extend the probability of lower taxicity and produce a hundred megacuba campaign speech."

"You have not mentioned civil rights."

"Without regard to space, need or choler."

"Then the ideal party is——?"

"——the party that has not lost faithinamerica, the party that sees the initiative, that can implement achievement and achieve implementation, that can close the gap, definitize the image, initiate departures. The party with the ility, ism, idity and ment required to realize the vision."

"Amazing how pleasing and lulling these sounds! My mental capacity and inquisitive posture are undergoing significant reduction and the deceleration of wit is proceeding on an alarming order of magnitude, sir, and yet you have neglected to assure, before the onset of inertia, that this great Republic will be maintained secure from those who would destroy it, from within as well as without."

"Sleep well, citizen, Government of the peephole by the peephole shall not perish from this earth."

POLITICS AND POVERTY

"Good evening, ladies and gentlemen of the radio audience and welcome to another network mini-chat, the program that brings America two minutes of elevating thought by our nation's most elevated thinkers. Our talk tonight is by the noted Administration economist, Professor Ian Klugg. Dr. Klugg."

"Thank you and good evening. You must all have heard at some time recently these criticisms that the Administration has failed to get the country moving again. Just last spring, you recall, there was an extraordinary upsurge of press interest in the poor, with the rather unfair implication that your Government had very little sympathy for the miserable conditions under which millions of Americans live in the midst of general affluence.

"Actually, nothing could be further from the truth. Your Government is deeply concerned with the alarming persistence of poverty and joblessness and, what is more, it is doing everything possible to restore full economic vitality.

"In passing, I might point out that this Administration has fought two political campaigns on the issue of providing decent medical care for the aged poor. I am certain that we will again be on the side of the aged poor during the campaign of 1964. And, indeed, during the campaigns of 1966 and 1968.

"There are, of course, political and economic difficulties complicating the issue. The doctors and health-insurance companies feel that these aged indigents should be provided for in a manner more consistent with the traditional profit motive.

"This is an issue on which decent men may honorably disagree. We happen to side with the poor, but we must concede that the ideal solution would be to strengthen the overall economy so that everyone can pay his own doctor bill.

"For this reason, we are asking the poor to be patient awhile longer while we concentrate our energies on our tax-revision bill, now just emerging from the House Ways and Means Committee. Here we have sought to strike at the vicious taproot of poverty and unemployment by creating more incentives to business investment and giving the working chap a tax cut.

"Admittedly, the Ways and Means Committee has rewritten our program, but it is grossly unfair to say, as some people have done, that they have recast it as a 'rich man's bill.' We concede that if you happen to be comfortably well-to-do, you are going to be rather more pleased about this bill than if you are the sort who doesn't know what a capital gain is.

"But the essential fact about the tax bill is that it is a long step forward. It should certainly create a mood of ebullience in the upper-income brackets—and make them turn to the great engines of production and investment with new zest.

"Of course, we do not expect miracles overnight. The Senate will delay the bill for another year, and after that the anticipated benefits may be somewhat slow to trickle down, but on the whole we can justifiably say that movement ahead has begun.

"In the meantime, you will say, we are making no progress at all toward reducing unemployment, and the statistics would seem to bear you out. What is often overlooked, however, is the really impressive number of these unemployed who are too old for jobs in the new industries, or young people freshly out of school who can be supported by parents.

"We are making a major effort to cut unemployment among youngsters freshly out of school by urging them to go back to school. If we can persuade the youth of this country to keep going back to school for each of the next five years, unemployment can be held within acceptable limits until 1969 when we go out of office.

"In closing, let me say that it is easier to find fault with your Government, particularly if you have been out of work a year or two, than it is to solve these very difficult problems. And so, for that wretched minority of you who feel forgotten, I urge you to consider going back to school. Good night."

THE TAXPAYER'S DOLLAR

This place is full of mystery men. Recently, for example, after the House had chopped down the foreign-aid bill, *The Washington Post* reported that "one member" said Congress was sending President Johnson up to the U.N. "with his coattails cut off."

This is the kind of felicitous commentary we have learned to expect of the ubiquitous "one member," but who is this mystery man who keeps illuminating the Congressional news like a Greek chorus?

Insiders—that's Irving Insiders, another Washington mystery man—will not say. No matter. It can be—Harry Itcanbe, the State Department leak artist—revealed that "one member" is actually a pseudonym for the mysterious Ernie Onemember.

Ernie Onemember, of course, is not a Congressman at all, but an incorrigible phrasemaker who ingratiates himself with reporters by coining mean comments about Congress and telling its ugliest secrets. He is not, as commonly supposed, related to the pseudonymous "One Wag," who goes around town telling jokes on the Government.

"One Wag" is actually the brilliant philosopher and wit, Wun Wag, who escaped from mainland China in 1950. Friends call him "Wags" and recite his aphorisms in the style of old "Confucius say" jokes. In fact, Onemember's latest *mot* may have been filched from Wun Wag. "Wags say Congress sending President Johnson to U.N. with coattails cut off" sounds more like the old philosopher than the garrulous Onemember.

These are all lesser mystery men, of course. Many Washingtonians have at one time or another had a drink or dined with Ernie Onemember, Irv Insiders, Harry Itcanbe and old Wags. The fellow that everybody in town is dying to see unmasked—the real mystery man of this city—is The Taxpayer.

Though nobody has ever seen The Taxpayer, everyone is certain that he exists. Some time ago, it seems the Government took a dollar from him. Ever since then, the city has been half-crazed with the fear that somebody will use The Taxpayer's dollar badly.

What makes it impossible to discover The Taxpayer's identity is that nobody is willing to admit he has never seen The Taxpayer. Politicians insist that they know what The Taxpayer wants done with his dollar. Pundits are constantly saying that The Taxpayer is unhappy about the plans for his dollar.

These people would have us believe that they are so cosy with The Taxpayer that they can speak his mind with authority. If so, why does The Taxpayer tell them all something different?

No, these people obviously do not know who The Taxpayer is either. If pressed for an introduction, they become irritated and reply with some nonsense like, "Everybody is The Taxpayer."

It is impossible to see how everybody can be The Taxpayer. For one thing, The Taxpayer is perpetually urging politicians not to spend his dollar on this or that group of people.

When the Pentagon said it was closing some superfluous bases to save The Taxpayer's dollar, all sorts of people complained. These complainers were clearly out of sympathy with The Taxpayer. In fact, some of their Congressmen asserted that these very complainers were The Taxpayer.

Whoever he is, The Taxpayer obviously speaks with a forked tongue. To keep him satisfied, for example, the President ordered a full day's work in Government offices last

Christmas Eve. Although Government workers pay taxes, they apparently have no influence with The Taxpayer.

That evening The Taxpayer was sitting home hissing Ebenezer Scrooge for trying to get a shilling's value out of Bob Cratchit for a shilling spent, but by twelfth night seven senators had reported him outraged about wasting The Taxpayer's dollar on welfare schemes.

What a curious animal he must be, speaking with his forked tongue and weeping crocodile tears. Miniaturized in plastic, he would make a nice Christmas toy for small children. "There is no such animal," the children would say.

The Taxpayer would probably buy them in hundred-thousand lots. At a dollar apiece.

PRESIDENT-WEARY

April, 1964—The great question facing America this spring is not, "How does Lyndon Johnson keep it up?" but, "How long can the rest of us stand it?"

The problem is poignantly expressed in a letter from a Washington woman who writes, "All my husband and I can do in the evenings nowadays is sit around talking about Lyndon Johnson." Others report similar problems.

Some people are so alarmed about the amount of time the President occupies in their minds that they shut themselves in padded rooms and concentrate on not thinking about Lyndon Johnson. They usually come out of seclusion screaming for the latest papers to see what he has done between editions.

There is always something. He has stretched a beagle's ears, pioneered a new teleprompter, jollied a King, broken the speed limit, done the fox trot, inspired the poor, made the trains run, charmed the businessmen, shown the Rose Garden, flown to Chicago, written to Khrushchev, thrown a light switch, granted boons to a six-year-old, tossed out the first ball, lobbied a Senator, greeted the tourists.

For the first time in anyone's memory, we have a President who does everything. There is something to be said for such a President, but there are also drawbacks. In the past, it was customary for the burdens of the office to wear out our Presidents; now we have a President who threatens to wear out the country.

The question President Johnson should ask himself is whether it is altogether healthy for everybody to have to think about a President all the time. A President is admittedly an important man, but when all is said and done he is still only a President.

Right now, for example, it is very hard to get in any concentrated thinking about Khrushchev, De Gaulle, Princess Irene, Elizabeth Taylor, the New York Mets, Sam Huff. All of these institutions keep appearing at the edge of the news, waiting to be thought about, as they should be thought about in any well-balanced society.

Lyndon Johnson won't give them a chance. Just as the mind comes to grips with Khrushchev's denunciation of the birthday greeting he received from Mao Tse-tung, Lyndon Johnson commandeers the television screen to announce that he has done a good deed for Cathy May.

The "Cleopatra" interests sue Elizabeth Taylor, but before the mind can relax for a bit of light spring thinking Lyndon Johnson has pounced all over page one with prophecies of nirvana just around the corner.

It is only a guess, of course, but it is doubtful if the average conscious American these days can go for more than two minutes without thinking of Lyndon Johnson. Is this really good politics?

When General Eisenhower was President, he often let people go for three or four weeks at a stretch without intruding into their lives. The voters loved him, perhaps because he let them alone.

With his big family, President Kennedy was fortunate. There were enough Kennedys making news to guarantee that everybody would have to think of one Kennedy or another every day, and the variety of personalities kept Kennedy-think from becoming tiresome.

President Johnson seems bent on retaining every second of public thought that was once spread out through the entire Kennedy family—John and his father, the Ambassador, Robert, Teddy, Sargent Shriver, Jacqueline, Ethel, Eunice, Jean, Caroline and John, Jr. It is an incredible task. No one but Lyndon Johnson could have done it. But can the country take it?

If Mr. Johnson holds the pace, the weaker links in the electorate will surely start screaming for mercy before Election Day, and by 1968 the whole country will be mentally exhausted.

Take a week at the ranch, Mr. President. Bar the gates. Doze by the pool. Give us all a chance to rediscover Casey Stengel, to ponder the mystery of Harold Stassen and to dream of the glories of Sophia Loren.

COCKTAILS JOHNSON STYLE

The sound of the Washington cocktail party varies from year to year, from season to season. In February 1964 it sounded like this:

"Well, I've never been so thrilled in my life. I mean, just like that, he came out and said, 'Would you like to see what the second floor looks like?' Well, you have no idea of what it's like, my dear, to stand in the Lincoln bedroom and think that Lincoln himself, right there in that very room. . . ."

"Waiter! Don't they have any branchwater at this place? Branchwater, man. Branchwater. That's what they drink with it in Texas. . . ."

"Well, Harry and I have this little place out in Virginia,

near Winchester, you know. It's not much, but it's our own little ranch, you know, and I don't know what would happen to Harry's ulcer without it. . . ."

"Hi, there, y'all. What's this I hear about you selling your French expressionists and buying a herd with the proceeds?"

"Impressionists, Joe John. French impressionists. Well, we'd put a lot of money in those paintings and the fact is we just got tired of having them around. We weren't really seeing them any more, you know. Then, after Lyndon's State of the Union message, I said to the bride here, 'Why don't we sell off those pictures and invest in something we can watch grow . . . ?"

"What a blast! I hear the President's going to address us over a telephone hook-up after the thousandth guest arrives."

"Harry, do we really have to drink this bourbon and branchwater every time when we go out? Two-thirds of this mob hasn't the faintest notion that it was Sam Rayburn's favorite drink."

"Good evening, Mr. Secretary. Oh, yes, sir, we're old bourbon-and-branchwater drinkers from way back. I see by the papers you've been down at the ranch."

"Yes. Wonderful place for a man to get away from all this Washington tension and artificiality and feel the American earth under his feet."

"I guess you feel the strength of the soil flowing right into your pores when you get your feet into that earth and look up at those glittering stars."

"Yes, indeed, you can see why the President has to get back there ever so often. I know it sounds corny, but this man really soaks up America through his pores. Don't misunderstand me about Jack Kennedy, now. American culture-wise, he was unsurpassed, but this man's ability to breathe America in through his pores is astounding. . . ."

"All right, waiter. I know it's a pitcher of martinis and not a pitcher of branchwater, but I'll try it anyhow."

"Listen, Tom Pete, you and I know the University of Texas is just as good as Harvard, but what we've got to do is prove it to all these Schlesingers. . . ." "Harry, why do all Texans have two first names?"

"Let's ask old Joe John over there."

"That isn't Joe John, Harry. That's Bill Don Pete. I recognize him from his picture in the society page, and we haven't even been introduced to him. . . ."

"Listen, baby, why don't we get away from all these squares from the prairie and go over to my flat and have things the way they used to be. Candlelight and some art talk. I'll slip into a tab-collar shirt and one of my old ivy league suits. . . ."

"Waiter, bring me another pitcher of that branchwater pronto! Senator, this man soaks up America through his pores. I say he ought to face up to De Gaulle and exude all that America that's in him, and let's see then how De Gaulle comes off in a Gallup poll against him."

"And, baby, for old time's sake I'll show you my print of the Mona Lisa. . . ."

"Look, all that happened was this friend of mine called up and said how would I like to buy a little of this new stock. What's so wrong about that, especially when I've never even met Bobby Baker . . . ?"

"Harry, where have you been?"

"On the phone, darling. Darling, you won't believe this. . . . I mean, it's crazy, but guess who just now on the telephone. . . .

PART 7

TEARS FOR SOME OLD FRIENDS

SAM SPADE & CO.

Look at what is happening to our old friend, the private eye. He is turning into a clotheshorse. It is absurd and sad.

Absurd because these new sissified private eyes, with their marcelled hair and cashmere jackets, obviously couldn't get the goods on a hub-cap snatcher. Sad because the private eye, like the cowboy, has always been an expression of the American male's daydreams about himself as rogue hero.

If the new private eyes personify the American man's dream of masculinity, the American woman needs help. Sam Spade wasn't a man that a woman could hold, but she wasn't likely to forget him. He was mean, unpressed, hung over and ill-mannered, but he had a Roman contempt for the softness of the society that used him.

Raymond Chandler's hero, Philip Marlowe, was an alienated romantic making a lonely stand for individualism. He was scruffy and perhaps more high-principled than a woman could afford, but he was a man. Even that dim-witted troglodyte, Mike Hammer, whom we owe to Mickey Spillane, had muscle to commend him.

The striking difference about the new boys is that they are all insiders. They are never mad at the system. They know how to make the system work for them. They are in with the cops, in with the big-money crowd, in with the blondes. The old boys were outsiders fighting the system. They were lone guns taking those awful beatings for peanut fees, and they operated on the rebel's theory that the good things of life—duplex apartments, sports cars, racy dames and Tattersall vests—cost more in compromise than they could honorably pay.

Not the new boys. You see them on television, the contemporary supplier of the nation's escape fiction, living as high as the Medici. One group, with sybaritic headquarters at 77 Sunset Strip, frequents the most chichi night clubs. Another operates from a quarter-million-dollar boat anchored at Miami Beach.

Honolulu harbors a group known as "Hawaiian Eyes." They spend a lot of time in Polynesian restaurants combing their hair and sipping perfumed booze through gardenias. None of these boys would dream of meeting Sam Spade for beer in a one-armed lunchroom.

Their women are not dames; they are dreamboats spun of college boys' fantasies. Spade would have spanked them, scrubbed their faces and carried them home to rich old father. The new boys take them to Polynesian resturants and introduce them to the bartender.

As devout insiders, the new private eyes believe in self-indulgence. They are tailored to break a dreamboat's heart. Their coiffures are the most gorgeously barbered, their cars the sportiest.

The cops, with whom they enjoy the new togetherness, have been cleaned up and slimmed down until they are indistinguishable from the private eyes. One such cop operates —believe it or not—from a Rolls-Royce. He is as debonair as Porfirio Rubirosa.

There is another TV cop, who has been to college and is always amazing his chief with his grasp of psychology.

The result since the cops and the private eyes have merged identities is neither convincing cop nor convincing private eye any longer. All we have left is a bunch of boy detectives trained not on *The Police Gazette* but on *Playboy Magazine*.

Would any sane millionaire send these boys up against Sidney Greenstreet and Peter Lorre to recover the Maltese Falcon or the Brasher Doubloon? Their milieu is not the alley behind Mr. Big's casino, but the Bunny Club; their forte is not absorbing a murderous beating from a team of gorillas, but sending the martini back for more gin.

Surely these boys cannot be the contemporary American male's daydream of masculinity. Or can they? Sam Spade would have spanked them, torn up their Playmate albums, and taken them home to dad.

JACK ARMSTRONG

A young man who works in a large Washington office reports that during a late-afternoon lull recently he noticed a strange incident.

Returning from a circuitous trip to the water cooler, he passed through an area of desks where five of his older co-workers—a woman and four men in their late thirties and early forties—were taking turns singing. He was puzzled because none of the tunes seemed familiar, and it was only after considerable application that he understood what was happening.

"They were singing old radio commercials," he explained. "Stuff they remembered from children's shows on radio back in the early 1930's. One would start singing one of these vintage commercials, and then another would come in and correct a word or add a line or polish up the tune a little."

The youngish man, who must have been born about 1939, was fascinated. "None of them could remember more than the first two lines of the theme song for 'Jack Armstrong, the All-American Boy,' " he said. "These went:

" 'Wave the Flag for Hudson High, boys.

" 'Show them how we stand.'

"All of them remembered, though, that the announcer introducing the show always said, 'Jack Armstrong. The Alllllllllll-American Boy,' dragging out 'all' in a long chant."

Everyone, he said, also seemed to have total recall on the Tom Mix show's commercial, a paean to Ralston cereal.

"Ask your mother in the morning, to serve you up a steaming plate. It's grand hot whole-wheat cereal, and the cowboys think it's great. Once you try it, then you'll buy it, 'cause it's really swell to eat. Jane and Jimmy, too, say it's good for you. Ralston cereal can't be beat."

"It was eerie," the younger man said. "Here were these middle-aged brains playing back old advertising that had been stored in them when they were anywhere from six to ten years old. Some of that stuff must have come out of the radio when Hoover was still President.

"One of the men remembered that you could get cowboy chaps for boxtops from H-O oatmeal, whatever that was. Another said he had once gotten an Orphan Annie decoder by sending away boxtops and complained that children nowadays don't have enough drive to save boxtops the way he did.

"Another fellow gave an imitation of the sound effect for a rocketship blastoff on Buck Rogers, which everybody said was very good. A graying man tried to hum the theme music from 'Chandu the Magician' without much success. He could not remember it very well, he said, because 'Chandu' came on a 8 P.M. and he was never allowed up that late except on Fridays."

The session ended when a minor executive swung into view and the celebrants of old radio resumed paper shuffling.

What impressed the younger man was the example of how durable a commercial can be when it is inserted into the young mind. What is more likely to impress anyone in the thirty-five to forty-five age group is the bond of shared memories that links him to the invisible empire of Depression children. Memories of boxtops hoarded for secret decoders, of Tom Mix telling the Wrangler to saddle up Tony, of Killer Kane and Ardala holding Doctor Huer prisoner on the planet Jupiter.

Surely, everybody remembers Buck Rogers' brainy adviser, Doctor Huer. He had that great domed skull, denoting an intelligence capable of whipping up a disintegrator-gun neutralizer on an impulse, and he had that little scrub mustache. People who don't remember Doctor Huer weren't really molded by the Depression. They may be older people who suffered through it or youngsters who missed it, but they are not its own children.

Those who are held together by shared memories of Doctor Huer and the Wrangler and Chandu are likely to feel sentimental about it in retrospect and not at all angry with the old ad men who cluttered their minds with chants to Ralston, Ovaltine and H-O oats.

Naturally, they are not so relaxed about the memories their own children are acquiring nowadays from the ad man and the TV tube. What messages will the children be able to play back in 1994? We can't foresee, thank goodness. We can only hope that they will retain nothing worse than Killer Kane and Ardala holding old Huer on the planet Jupiter and a few old commands to buy Ralston, H-O oats and Ovaltine.

THE MEAN MEN

On the day that Peter Lorre died, "The Outer Limits," a contemporary TV horror show, was doing a play which represented evil as a tremulous blob of gelatin.

The gelatin had lured a typical group of life's losers into an old dark house and, from time to time, forced them up to his room where he picked their brains, as it were, by invading their skulls with powerful extrasensory emanations. The gelatin is clearly evil, as well as ugly, but it is evil in the ambiguous modern way that children may sense but not explain.

The thing is torturing its captives in order to improve its knowledge of human beings. Symbolically, it might be modern science, playing its inhumane practical jokes to get amusing reactions, or it might be the modern superstate in its sleepless quest for new methods to dehumanize the living.

Those who remember Peter Lorre's film villainies will probably recall him fondly for years to come. Children cutting their teeth on today's gelatinous villains are not so fortunate.

The Lorre generation of villains thrived in a national atmosphere of simple optimism. They catered to the comfortingly simple faith that a certain percentage of the human race was just no good.

It was accepted that mean men sat around in dim rooms cackling up foul plots to get hold of the Maltese Falcon, and that they did it out of pure greed, cussedness and contempt for the law. The straight-shooters always won, of course.

The audience took its deepest satisfaction from the wretched deaths of the mean men, which underlined the moral, and the greatest and most beloved villains were those who could die with high style. Edward G. Robinson, rolling down the church steps with three slugs in the digestive tract, epitomized the rat whom you could recall with affection.

Most of them are gone now—Sidney Greenstreet, Lorre's fat partner in crime; Laird Cregar, whose final throes always expressed such regret for his misspent lives. Others have been put out of the villain business by modern history, which has put individual villainy out of fashion.

Robert Preston, one of the nastiest fellows who ever wore a black hat, and Anthony Quinn, the former treacherous redskin, have gone respectable. Boris Karloff is making lovable jokes about his past. And worst of all, Edward G. Robinson, is doing parodies of "Little Caesar" in a TV commercial for instant coffee.

The mean men were succeeded briefly by the Nazis, who either shouted "Wunderbar!" when informed that Errol Flynn was to have his mustache plucked at Gestapo headquarters, or whined "I don't vant to go back to Chermany" after their explosive pencils had been seized by James Cagney.

The Nazis were not merely mean men. They were symbols of the more depressing assumption that whole nations were mean. From this point, villainy went to the Freudian stage. Suddenly there was no such thing any longer as mean men. There were only sick men.

Villainy reached its nadir in this era when Hitchcock sent Gregory Peck stalking Ingrid Bergman with a razor in his hand. It was laughable to be asked to believe that good old Peck might be Laird Cregar in gaunt clothing.

And now the age of the evil gelatin. It is marked by a procession of sinister blobs, ugly machines, faceless tripeds, giant crabs, bodiless emanations from evil galaxies and, in its more sophisticated forms—as "Dr. Strangelove," "The Spy Who Came in from the Cold" and "Seven Days in May"—whole earthbound governments and political movements.

In common, all are dehumanized and disembodied. Their malice, whether incidentally or by design, is directed against the human being, usually out of some incomprehensible scheme by some inhuman system with good intentions.

It is a bit too like life to be entertaining. When a system is destroying you with good intentions, the predicament is too complex to be solved by pumping three slugs into its digestive tract on the church steps. We have missed Peter Lorre for longer than we realize.

PART 8

AN ASSORTMENT OF CELEBRATIONS

TO RISE ABOVE BLAZE STARR

December 31, 1963—We, the undersigned, hereby resolve as follows:

I. That during the year 1964 we will live more courageously and, to this end, will therefore:

(a) Discontinue the craven practice of tipping hatcheck girls who threaten to call the manager unless we surrender our coats, bartenders who serve two-ounce olives in three-ounce martini glasses, waiters who hate their profession, and cab drivers who harangue us with tales of the miserly tips given by the cheapskates who just got out of their taxis;

(b) Admit, whenever challenged, that we do not know the difference between a flanker back and a tight end, that our automobiles are getting only nine miles to the gallon, that we do not understand the Common Market, that we have not read "The Affluent Society," and that we cannot ski, skin-dive, dance or read a French menu; and,

(c) Create unpleasant scenes when barbers cut our hair badly, when airlines overbook our flights, when parking-lot attendants dent our fenders, when hotel clerks say it is impossible to honor our reservations.

II. That during the year 1964 we will at last genuinely undertake a course of self-improvement and, to this end, will therefore:

(a) Finally read "A Tale of Two Cities," "Silas Marner," "The Idylls of the King," "Remembrance of Things Past," "Finnegans Wake" and the "Scarlet Letter";

(b) Walk, instead of drive, at least once each week to the drugstore for cigarettes;

(c) Learn to identify birds, flowers, shrubs, trees and the colors of women's clothing by correct name or adjective;

(d) Learn to tell a Bordeaux from a Burgundy without reading the label and tell Bach from Stravinsky without peeking at the record jacket; and,

(e) Make the casual acquaintance of science by finding out what the following really mean: a laser, binary numbers, DNA, polyunsaturated fats, Gardol and aerospace systems.

III. That during the year 1964 we will practice humility and tolerance and, to this end, will therefore:

(a) Admit that we are not very good drivers; quit insisting that our capacity for alcohol, and for almost everything else, is just as good as it used to be; have our eyeglasses strengthened; concede that Roger Maris can hit better than we can; think of something nice to say about Richard Nixon; and, when scolding the children, remember that while age occasionally brings wisdom it often just hardens the arteries.

IV. That during the year 1964 we will toughen our characters by surmounting problems toward which we have hitherto taken the line of least resistance and, to this end, will therefore:

(a) Make a determined effort to get two tickets to "My Fair Lady" at box-office prices;

(b) See "Cleopatra";

(c) Get into a world series game without using influence; and,

(d) Master the history of the Congo, from Lumumba to Adoula, and develop an opinion about U.N. policy there.

V. And finally, that during the year 1964 we will strive to become more fully developed citizens with a greater awareness of the world around us and, to this end, will therefore:

(a) Make a conscientious effort to find out what is going on in Laos and where it is, what it is that Nikita Khrushchev is chairman of, and what happened to the Kurdish revolt in Iraq;

(b) Do our best to become interested in the activities of Tom Mboya, Princess Grace, Wilt Chamberlain, the Gabor sisters, George Romney, Kwame Nkrumah, Charles Percy, Dirk Stikker, the Beatles, Bourke B. Hickenlooper and Ava Gardner; and,

(c) Cut down on the disproportionate amount of time devoted to Groucho Marx, Dick Tracy, Vince Lombardi, Sophia Loren, Casey Stengel, Blaze Starr, Jack Daniels, Danny Kaye and Perry Mason.

All who subscribe to these articles should, of course, be warned that they will probably regret it.

THE MEGADAFFODIL BOMBSHELL

Spring came to Washington this week. Naturally there was a cocktail reception for her. Everybody went. It was the thing to do. She had mud on her skirts and a sprig of forsythia in her wind-blown hair.

"She looks to me like a slut," said an immaculate young matron whose husband does something classified in the State Department. From across the room, under eyelids the hue of crocus lavender, Spring winked. She was lovely. She made you want to tousle the hair of immaculate young matrons all over Georgetown.

The impulse to do something for her was overpowering—to buy her offerings of fragrant white lawn lime and hemlock food, to present her with gleaming new pruning shears and a quatrain. "Oh, she's handsome enough," conceded a brilliant young thinker from the Pentagon, "but what I'd like to know is whose side she would really be on if things came to a showdown."

"Surely you don't think—"

"The fact is that she is impartially arming the Soviet Union and Communist China with the gloom deterrent just as casually as though they were elements of the free world. Try to imagine how many megadaffodils are already sprouting in the Caucasus and Ukraine," said the brilliant young thinker. He exuded the faint odor of intercontinental-ballistic-missile grease and computer lint.

Spring answered by plucking a blue jay from her hair and giggling. A Senator who was stuffing on shrimp said that he had nothing against Spring, although he doubted that a restaurant owner could be legally compelled to serve her against his will, as the Founding Fathers had not seen fit when drawing the Constitution to state, either explicitly or by implication—

Spring blew him a kiss, scattering the mummy dust out of his eyebrows. An investigator from the Bobby Baker case whispered that the two had been seen together last year at the Kentucky Derby.

An inscrutable White House source drifted by. "The President would rather not see a lot of irresponsible talk in the press about Spring," he said, "until the Administration has firmly decided on policy." It can be reliably reported, however, that the President has not told Spring to stay out of Wisconsin and has not, as some reports have it, refused to give Spring an appointment.

The White House source was closely followed, as usual, by friends of the Attorney General, who said that there was no substance to reports of a feud between their man and Spring, no matter what the inscrutable White House source was saying. Spring snickered gustily and rattled the trash cans to show her indifference to the whole Democratic ticket.

"The problem," said a State Department gentleman, "is not whether Spring will wear the daring new empire bustline, but whether she will move us toward realization of the multilateral nuclear force.

"This sentimentality about Spring the Eternal is quite touching, of course," he explained, "but is it really any more eternal than De Gaulle? The trouble, you see, is that it is very difficult to exert leverage against these eternal phenomena and, hence—" Spring summoned a small rain cloud and emptied its contents lightly on the State Department man's pate, reminding him abruptly that life was for living.

Most of the better people by this time had backed Spring into a corner and were asking ridiculous questions. What did she think of the New Hampshire voting and whom would the Republicans run for President? Wasn't it terrible about Cassius Clay's joining the Black Muslims? Had she heard of the outrageous speech of Malcolm X? What did she think of the minimal-deterrent theory, and about saturation parity?

Spring turned green, produced a tulip shoot out of her sleeve, tipped an elm with buds and showed them a swarm of termites dancing in a shaft of sunlight. It was old stuff, tired miracles and familiar flummery when what was needed was hot dope, cool opinion and powerful answers.

The guests soon lost interest, and while Spring stood indifferent in the sunlight some young men and young women drove by in a hot rod and pelted her with beer cans.

THE NAME OF THE GAME IS SPRING MADNESS

"The defendant will state his name."

"Bauer, your Honor. Hank Bauer."

"Your profession, Mr. Bauer?"

"Baseball, your Honor. I manage the Baltimore Orioles."

"That, I take it, is the same corporation which does business under the names of 'The Birds,' 'The Flock' and 'The O's.' "

"Correct, your Honor."

"The clerk will read the charge."

"The baseball fans of America, hereinafter referred to as 'the fans,' do charge that in or about the final week of March 1964 Hank Bauer, alias 'The Old Marine,' manager of the

Baltimore Orioles, otherwise known as 'The Birds,' 'The Flock' and 'The O's,' did willfully violate the baseball code in that said Bauer, under questioning by sports writers, otherwise known as 'the scribes,' refused to predict that The Birds would win the American League pennant and stated as his opinion that they would finish no higher than third."

"Grave charges, Mr. Bauer. You realize that the code of baseball states explicitly what managers must say when scribes question them?"

"Yes, your Honor. I know all those answers."

"Do you indeed? Let us see. Suppose a scribe asked, 'Hank, who is the greatest centerfielder you ever saw in action?' What is the answer?"

"I say, 'Joe DiMaggio.' "

"No, you do not say 'Joe DiMaggio,' Mr. Bauer. You say, 'That's easy. It has to be Joe.' Let me hear you say it correctly."

"That's easy. It has to be Joe."

"Yes. That gives the scribe the cue to write, 'The Old Marine was referring, of course, to the incomparable DiMag.' You see, Mr. Bauer, there is a good reason for everything in the code. Each spring the fans expect The Old Marine to help the scribes write their annual tributes to the incomparable DiMag. This sort of tradition hallows the game. Gives it roots in the past. Another question."

"Yes, sir?"

"What do you say when a scribe asks, 'Can the Yankees be beaten this year?' "

"I say, 'The Yankees are always tough, but the name of the game is breaks, and if the Yankees get a couple of bad breaks like Elston Howard breaking his hip and Mickey Mantle quitting the game, this could be a wide-open race.' "

"No, Mr. Bauer. You haven't done your homework. I'll read you the correct answer from the official code: 'Don't kid yourself, fellas, the Yankees can be taken by any one of five or six teams in this League. With the power we've added in the winter trades, and if a couple of our kid pitchers come around all right, and if we can lick our problems at shortstop and in the bullpen, we could be right in there all the way.' "

"Yes, your Honor."

"Now, how should you answer when asked to predict who will win the pennant?"

"I say, 'Don't count out the O's.' "

"No, Mr. Bauer. What you say is, 'This year we've got the material to take all the marbles.' "

"But, your Honor, it is very hard to take all the marbles when playing in the same league with the Yankees."

"Of course, Mr. Bauer, but you must never let the fans believe it. Everything in the code is there for good reason. You must convince the fans that this year The Birds have the material to take all the marbles. Should they fail, the fans will say, 'Since The Birds had the material to take all the marbles but didn't, it's the manager's fault.' "

"But that's the way to get myself fired, your Honor."

"Right, Mr. Bauer, but as it is much easier to find new managers than new players who really can take all the marbles, your firing will be good for baseball. Under a new manager the fans will come back next year with hope rejuvenated."

"What can I say, your Honor?"

"Say you were misquoted by the scribes. Say, 'It's The Birds for sure in '64.' And if you come back here on another code-violation charge, I'll give you five years with the Mets."

CHERCHEZ LA SEASHORE

WASHINGTON, *August, 1962*—A visitor from a rational land interviews an authoritative Administration spokesman on the August problem.

Q. You are an authoritative Administration spokesman?

A. Quite so. I have worked up through the ranks, serving

first as A Highly Placed State Department Source, then as A Veteran Capitol Observer and, most recently, as An Unimpeachable Authority at the Pentagon. I hope soon to be promoted to the rank of Authoritative White House Source.

Q. What is the Administration's position on August?

A. August has always been a bad time for all Administrations, but we believe it is, nevertheless, a month in which we can move ahead. In any case, we must not succumb to August and stand still.

Q. Since this is not for attribution, could you put away those cue cards from the Democratic National Committee and speak candidly?

A. Well, as you know, the French have always had the proper approach to August. They close down the Government, stop business, put up the shutters in Paris, and everybody goes to the seashore. They recognize that August distorts reason and wilts the spirit. They shun August. In this country, of course, August is even steamier, more enervating, dispiriting and deleterious to good sense than in France, but we Americans do not believe in surrendering to it.

Q. Why do Americans believe it is better to fight August than to enjoy it?

A. Very difficult to say. Perhaps it's our national Puritan zest for a good bout of the miseries. In any case, we insist on carrying on. Here, for example, we will soon have another Wayne Morse filibuster in the Senate if I'm not mistaken. A sure August phenomenon. Then, we can expect Representative Otto E. Passman to emasculate the foreign-aid bill. Another regular August event. The Russians have already started the latest round of nuclear tests before August is even well begun. The New York Yankees are turning the American League pennant race into a farce, as usual in August. Oh, I think you can expect things to get much worse before September.

Q. Do you have any theories why everything should go wrong in August?

A. Use your head, man. Would you strike out across the Sahara at high noon for a meditative stroll and expect to find wisdom? August deranges the brain. It is in August that dogs go mad, Scots see the Loch Ness monster, adolescents compete to see how many times they can toss an ice cube before it melts, Wayne Morse filibusters. . . . Don't quote me.

Q. Why doesn't any of this happen in July?

A. July is a high holiday of the spirit. It starts with fireworks. It is a season for catching lightning bugs and playing pinochle. But by August the crab grass is in charge and the Japanese beetle is in the roses. In July a subway is merely hot; in August it is a furnace. In July the air is merely humid; in August it is a steam that bastes the brain.

Q. Aren't you becoming slightly overwrought? Actually, August has produced great things. It was August, 1492, when Columbus sailed to discover America.

A. Hardly a happy event for Columbus. He expected to hit India, but where did he end up? The Dominican Republic. Here's the history of August for you, give or take a few days: August, A.D. 30, St. John the Baptist beheaded. St. Augustine died, August, A.D. 430. The young princes murdered in the Tower of London, August, 1483. August, 1566, Suleiman the Magnificent died. August, 1637, Ben Jonson died. August, 1769, Napoleon born. August, 1814, Washington captured by the British. August, 1914, World War I began. Hitler takes over Germany, August, 1934. August, 1945, the first atomic bombs dropped on people. Shall I go on?

Q. What is the answer to all this?

A. The French have the answer. Put up the shutters on Capitol Hill. Send Congress to the seashore. Let the President go sailing. A one-month moratorium on commerce in New York, Chicago, St. Louis and Los Angeles. Let everyone get into Bermuda shorts, pack the kids into the car and go to the seashore. Everybody at once. There would be a month of national quiet and introspection while the whole country studied the miraculous flow of the waves and tides and, at night, pondered the inaccessibility of Arcturus.

Q. Will the Administration sponsor legislation along this line?

A. You didn't hear me correctly. I said that the *French* had the answer to the problem. It so happens that the French believe that life is for living. Any Administration that propounded that philosophy in this country would find its Gallup rating down thirty points before the message reached Congress. The Administration wants the country to move, even in August when movement is so difficult and dangerous. No country can move when everybody has gone to the seashore.

Q. I'll bet I can quote you on that.

A. You certainly may. And on the way out, would you turn down that air conditioner? It's harder and harder to get warm around here.

MORE TO BE PITIED THAN FEARED

On the occasion of Halloween, let a good word be said for monsters. For Frankenstein's luckless electrified oaf. For Count Dracula in that uncomfortable winged collar. For the Wolf Man and his son, and for King Kong and his son, and for all the poor mummies dug out of Egypt.

They have never been properly understood, principally because of publicity agents and psychologists. The publicity agents always depicted them as horrors, and the psychologists warn against letting the children become too involved with them. Both views are wrong.

The common trait of all the really great monsters is their touching human simplicity. This is probably why they have endured so well and why they are so popular with children today. In most cases, they are simple romantics driven to distraction and then to violence by a human society which will not leave them in peace.

In the typical monster film, the truly monstrous deeds are done by the respectable citizenry against the monster. By urbane scientists working on the principle that anything goes in the quest for knowledge. By panicked lynch mobs of townspeople. By aggressive businessmen—as in King Kong—who mean to get rich at the monster's expense.

Consider the Frankenstein case. Here we have a gentle imbecile who likes to smoke cigars and hear the violin. He yearns for the simple life, but it is denied him by the bumbling scientist who created him and by an incompetent (and probably underpaid) lab technician.

They have stupidly outfitted the wretched fellow with a third-rate brain. Not content with that, they have left electrodes sticking out of his neck and have dressed him in a comically undersized suit. The thing goes out in search of friendship only to discover that there is nothing society fears and hates like a misfit.

Before long the bloodhounds are after him. The poor devil is wreaking havoc in his pathetic attempts to get away, and the mob destroys him. It is a parable of sorts about the nuclear age.

Count Dracula is a more complex case. Superficially, there seems little to be said for him. And yet he is basically a victim of misfortune. Something bit him; consequently, he cannot entirely die. He needs blood to eke out a drab existence which requires him to spend the sunlight hours in a coffin.

It quickly becomes apparent to the group of stuffed shirts entertaining him that he is a desperate case. But does the doctor offer to treat him at the blood bank? No.

Instead, he torments the Count with wolfsbane and mirrors. The Count is fighting for his life, and the doctor sneaks upon him at sleep and puts a stake in his heart. Is there a hidden comment here on medical care for the luckless?

The Wolf Man has much the same problem. Most of the time he is sweet, genial Lon Chaney Jr., but when the moon is full he grows face hair and becomes quite mad, due to an unfortunate old werewolf bite. The condition is pitiable, but in movie after movie Chaney is invariably shot by some colorless leading man to protect society against its unfortunates.

And Kong. Poor Kong. His need is the love of a good woman. His love is unrequited. He is too ugly. In the end, the whole weight of the Pentagon is brought down upon him as the Air Force guns him off the Empire State Building. So much for lovesick freaks.

The mummies also seek love. Usually they have been buried alive for several thousands of years and are dug up for the titillation of science. Naturally, their thoughts turn at once to women. Naturally the women are repelled. (Mummies lack all the social graces.) And society does the outcast in.

And so it always is with the monsters. They are not quite tragic figures, but only noble unfortunates. They are not terrifying, but only pitiable. If the children like them, it may be comforting evidence that the children can still pity.

May the monsters find society hospitable and good women romantic this Halloween.

TAPS FOR A LOST HOLIDAY

One of the saddest things that has ever happened to a holiday was the conversion of Armistice Day into Veterans Day. Of course, it was as logical as a corporate merger. After Korea, there were too many veterans of too many wars, and the decision was to consolidate honors for all in one single day.

And yet it was sad, for Armistice Day had been something far more special in this country than an occasion to honor the fighting men. For the longest time—well on into the nineteen-thirties when the well-informed already realized the hope was false—it was the day that marked the end of war. Not merely the end of the Great War, but the end of war.

A few seers knew better before even the Versailles Conference had ended, and some of the cynicism of the nineteen-twenties had filtered down by mid-Depression to the boys and girls who were learning the Big Apple on the drugstore corner. By the time you moved on from knickers to long pants, you knew enough, when consulted on politics, to say "Wilson was a good man, but he was an idealist." ("Idealism" in those days connoted a benign mental illness.) And the phrase "the war to end war" was always heavily inflected with irony.

Still, the hope that Wilson had created was a long time dying. If you sneered without quite knowing why when you spoke of "the war to end war," you nevertheless felt a peculiar emotion when, at 11 A.M. on Nov. 11, the teacher asked the class to stand for a minute of silence and the kid with not enough wind blew "taps" down in the schoolyard.

After school the veterans paraded down Main Street with their handsome khaki tunics buttoned over the Adam's apple and those old wraparound leggings. It was not until Pearl Harbor that the last American realized that Armistice Day had been a deception all along. Consolidating it into Veterans Day was an act of realism, a tacit admission concurred in by the country that war in one form or another was here to stay.

This act of recognition is usually regarded as part of the country's growing up, and is generally thought to be a sign of healthy maturity. Now we are all practicing successful adult living. What are the children doing after school now, forty-four years after the buglers blew "Cease Fire" along the Western Front?

Here they come now, home from school, bearing the usual collection of mimeographed instructions for parents. What have we today? It is a message from Carl F. Hansen, Superintendent of Washington public schools. Mr. Hansen is thinking about war. He is full of advice. His instructions include the following:

"Since no public school funds are available for the purchase of shelter supplies, parents will be asked to supply the funds necessary for stocks of food, water, and sanitation and health kits." Principals will let us know how big a check to write. They will buy an assortment of "survival biscuits," which "have a shelf life of five years and may be purchased in metal containers."

Good, but what is this, Mr. Hansen? "Maintain a spirit of confidence in the home in all matters relating to the cold war situation: . . . Too much stress upon the dangers of the situation as far as children are concerned can create feelings of insecurity."

Well, none of us wants to create feelings of insecurity in our children. We shall have to take steps to maintain more confidence around the house about the cold war situation. That will mean selling the television set and stopping the newspaper subscription.

What we need, obviously, is a national program to convince the children that nuclear war is impossible, that Hiroshima and Nagasaki were "the nuclear attacks to end nuclear attacks." Better yet, why not rehabilitate the old Armistice Day which contributed so much to the last generation's feelings of security?

But you say we've already done away with that because it was an unhealthy illusion of youth? Who's in charge of this world, anyhow?

THE MYLES STANDISH PAPERS

How long will the Government continue to suppress The Myles Standish Papers on the pretext that disclosure would impair the national security?

Captain Standish has been dead since 1656. Surely any secret details of his operations among the Massachusetts Indians during the establishment of the first Pilgrim colony will be of only limited interest to the Soviet Union. Yet, so long as his papers remain unpublished American scholarship is denied a trove of priceless information about the origins of Thanksgiving, the controversial John-Priscilla-Myles triangle and, most important of all, the real identity of this mysterious Elizabethan Englishman.

Assistant Secretary Arthur Sylvester, the Pentagon's chief

of information weaponry, answers all requests for publication by insisting he knows of no Standish Papers.

Now we know, of course, that The Myles Standish Papers do exist. We even know something of their faintly scandalous content. Captain Standish's appraisal of why the Pilgrim colony managed to survive, for example, can be quoted by every Harvard man in Georgetown: "Where the red Manne did erre most fatally was in giving us succoure instead of y-throwing us backe on the beache."

Those few who have had access to the papers also report that Standish's explanation of the first Thanksgiving differs markedly from the traditional histories. One version of his account circulating here reads as follows: "Seeing ourselves y-blessed with an abundance of goodes and marchandisable wherewithal, we bethought us to create a feaste of much jollitie and to invite the red Manne thereto. Thus did we seeke to imbue in him a boding of happinesse, in which estate of minde he might purchase fully of our abundance. Successe in this venture, we bethought us, would give an y-shot in the arme to Yuletide marchandising."

What little has leaked about Standish's account of his own origins is just enough to tantalize us. It seems certain, for example, that "Myles Standish" was merely a pseudonym and that "Standish" was, in fact, an extraordinarily sophisticated Englishman, perhaps a man of noble birth.

We can rule out the theory that he was really Francis Bacon, although the legend of his sending John Alden to ask for Priscilla's hand is entirely consonant with the way an Elizabethan intellectual would have courted an Irish girl of the lower classes. Bacon's presence in England, however, is indisputably documented until 1626, whereas "Standish" arrived in Massachusetts in 1620.

Here we are at the mercy of the few bureaucrats who have actually read The Myles Standish Papers in their entirety. We know that "Standish" twice compares his farm at Duxbury to the fields bordering the Avon in his native England. The papers are also said to suggest a strong sense of the theatrical in their author.

These are meager clues, but they suggest a conclusion too

significant to be ignored. If we assume that Bacon wrote Shakespeare and then fabricated Shakespeare's death in 1616 after tiring of playwriting, we are left with the question: What really happened to Shakespeare? Is it preposterous to believe that he went "underground" at Bacon's behest from 1616 until 1619, then reappeared to sign onto the Mayflower as "Myles Standish"?

We cannot be certain until the Pentagon releases The Myles Standish Papers for publication for scholarly study. Certainly, the probability that Shakespeare was one of the originators of the American Thanksgiving holiday should persuade the White House to publish at once.

JINGLE BELLS
1. *SANTA, GO FORTH*

Commencement address at graduation exercises from Santa Claus school:

"You men stand today at the threshold of life's greatest adventure. For one whole month you will be the living embodiment of childhood's sweetest dreams. To you will be granted the rare opportunity of lifting children's hearts and filling their little world with joy. Warm loving bundles of faith will cuddle upon your laps and whisper to you of dreams and aspirations they dare not confide even to their parents.

"How will you respond to this challenge? We here at Santa Claus A. & M. have no doubt that you will measure up to the highest standards so long as you abide by the precepts we have labored so hard to impart. Remember, these children will be completely in your power. Direct your every action to tighten your sway over their little minds.

"Let us always remember that attention to the small detail often distinguishes the great Santa Claus from the failure.

Keep your beards fitted tightly to the chin; nothing is more dispiriting than two inches of daylight showing between chin line and beard. Above all, we cannot caution you enough against yielding to tobacco and alcohol during rest periods behind the throne. There was a day when breath sweeteners could deceive your little visitors. Those days are gone.

"Many of you have complained about the severity of our laughing course. We realize how difficult it is these days to produce a good convincing 'Ho, Ho, Ho!' when we all feel such a powerful urge to sit down and cry. We can only suggest that you stop reading the newspapers for the next month.

"Many of you will note that a long series of 'Ho, ho, ho's' will bring on a spasm of racking coughs, particularly if the little visitor is pressing an elbow into your breastbone. In these cases a switch to 'Hah, hah, hah' usually relieves the problem. In no case, however, should you let out a 'Heh, heh, heh.' Most merchandisers feel that 'Heh, heh, heh' is extremely harmful to the store image.

"The great crisis each of you will face as Santa Claus is essentially one of morals. Here, each man must do what will permit him to live with his own conscience. We urge you once again, however, to be exceedingly careful in the commitments you place upon your little visitors' parents.

"I am sure that most of you would balk instinctively at agreeing to bring a chinchilla stole for some dewy-eyed six-year-old charmer or a real machine gun to a little boy of five. The marginal problem, however, arises with the toddler who climbs into your lap, smiles with angelic simplicity into your eyes and asks for his own private telephone or stereo rig.

"A bland commitment of this magnitude may occasionally produce ugly scenes with the parents and even violence. We suggest you consult your individual store manager for policy guidance, but as a loose rule of thumb we think it unwise to promise to bring anything that costs over $150 or requires regular professional maintenance service.

"And finally, a few simple do's and don'ts: Never flirt with the shopgirls while in uniform. After hours, do not frequent bars while wearing your Santa Claus suit. Keep the beard free at all times of soup and coffee stains. Keep an alert eye for parents trying to smuggle youngsters past your throne without paying a visit.

"In these cases, pick up your microphone and ask in a booming voice, 'Don't you want to come and tell Santa Claus what you want for Christmas? Heh, heh, heh'—I mean, 'Ho, Ho, Ho.'

"Graduates, go forth and take up the challenge that lies before you in the spirit with which the men of Santa Claus A. & M. have ever responded to Christmastide. Lift children's hearts. Fill their little world with joy. Light their childhood with a jolly 'Ho, ho, ho,' or at least a 'Hah, hah, hah.' The next four weeks are yours."

JINGLE BELLS *2. TRIAL BY CONSUMPTION*

The first Santas are out on the shopping-center tarmacs and the call to consume is heard in the land. Conscientious consumers have already flexed their revolving credit accounts and run their charge plates through preliminary heats at the department stores.

Sales are booming in toy departments and men's cosmetics. The signs are clear. When sales of plastic castles and bay rum rise, Christmas is on the wing. Orgiastic Christmas buying used to leave people feeling vaguely immoral, but morality must now take a back seat to economic necessity.

Economists now agree that the business of America is to consume. Consumption is the first civic duty of every man, woman and toddler. We now know that unless everybody keeps his consumption rate steadily increasing, the economy will stagnate, the Russians will beat us to the moon and Congress will be unable to afford its pay rise.

Accordingly, no consumer need feel uneasy about his commercial excesses this season. The goal is total consumption, and the man who balks may eventually have to explain why to a Congressional committee.

Women, who are shouldering the greatest part of the task, complain that since consuming became a patriotic duty, most of the joy has gone out of it. Typical of these gallant cold-war warriorettes is Mrs. A. X., who was recently interviewed at a toy counter:

"My, what a splendid little castle you've bought there, madam. Plastic, isn't it?"

"Yes. Modeled to scale on a real Bavarian castle, and only $1,799.95. I've worn my arches down looking for something more expensive, but this is the costliest thing I can find."

"You'll never meet your consumption quota at that rate, madam."

"Well, there are extras, of course. I can spend $179.99 for a two years' supply of genuine moat water imported from a real Bavarian castle."

"The children will like that."

"Yes, and for another $50 they'll ship it in aerosol cans. Then, I'll have to buy some small alligators to make the moat more realistic, and that means buying alligator feed and moat-water warmers to maintain it at subtropical temperature. Of course, the whole castle is terribly fragile, too."

"Yes, the children are sure to break it up before the moat-water supply runs out, and then you'll have to buy something else to replace it. Do you always shop with an eye for fragility?"

"Oh, yes. Buy shoddy, I say, if you want to buy American. When I first started consuming, I bought solid, substantial toys that the children had a terrible time destroying. Some years their Christmas toys would last the whole year. Another consuming season would come around, and the children didn't feel they needed anything. I had to smash their old toys myself to foster their consumptive urge."

"Shocking. You might have raised your children with underdeveloped consuming reflexes. What else do you plan to consume this Christmas?"

"Oh, you never plan. Planned consumption is almost as

stifling as buying with cash. What I do is get out early in the morning with nothing very clear in mind and wander through the stores buying as impulse strikes. Take this six-pack of bay rum I just bought my husband. If I'd thought about it in advance, I would have bought only a single bottle of bay rum. By waiting for an impulse, I raised my bay-rum consumption rate by a factor of six."

"But how do you pay for all this junk?"

"Renewed bank notes, refinanced mortgages, loans on the insurance, re-revolved credit accounts. Someday, somebody will want money, I suppose, but by that time somebody will have invented new refinancing methods to keep the country moving."

"You must feel extremely proud of the job you are doing for your country out here on the consuming line."

"Well, it isn't easy being on your feet all day, then going home to that awful mess of boxes, bags and wrapping cases, but somebody has to do it. I'm no heroine. I'm just a plain American housewife doing her duty."

JINGLE BELLS
3. *THE CURIOUS BING CROSBY*

December, 1962—It was awesome and a little spooky to hear those Venusian chimes echo across the cosmos from the transmitters of Mariner II Friday afternoon.

Here for the first time, earth was hearing the radio news bulletins from a planet next door. What goes on at 2:30 on a December Friday afternoon on Venus? Is there life there under the eternal clouds? If so, do Venusians realize that this is December, that there are precious few shopping days left until Christmas or that their planet is being scanned by a well-armed and exceedingly predatory neighbor with invasion on his mind?

The answers wait on the long job of decoding Mariner's chimes. In the meantime, let us speculate what Venusians might have learned if the Mariner expedition had been reversed and Venusians—why do we always think of Venusians as emerald green people?—had scanned earth for forty-two minutes on Friday afternoon.

Is it unreasonable to believe that after the chimes were decoded the green technologists might report something as follows?

"Temperature measurements of Earth's surface indicate a world meteorologically hostile to any form of life that might be recognizable to Venus. Two-thirds of the planet's surface is covered with a turbulent salty liquid uninhabitable by air-breathing creatures.

"Much of the limited land surface appears to be frozen wasteland. Mysterious blankets of white capable of supporting only the most primitive forms of life cover the South Pole and extend downward from the North Pole for a distance of perhaps 6,000 miles.

"In this zone, only the most primitive forms of life could survive the awful cold. Radio signals intercepted in the atmosphere indicate that, in fact, some primeval form of society may be struggling to exist in that incredibly hostile world. These creatures appear to have established a cult devoted to worshiping the white blanket they live on.

"Evidence to support this thesis lies in the mass of recorded radio data, most of which consists of a curious song that the earth creatures play constantly. In it, the singer says 'I'm Dreaming of a White Christmas,' which suggests a lamentation to propitiate the terrible white substance.

"The singer is invariably identified as something designated 'Bing Crosby.' What a Bing Crosby may be we can only speculate. Some of us believe it to be a living creature, perhaps a term which these primitive worshipers of the white substance use for all their singing priests.

"Atmospheric analyses reveal other terrible physical deterrents to the development of any advanced form of life.

Much of the air blanket enveloping the northern sector of the Western Hemisphere is a gaseous form of garbage compounded of lethal chemical wastes and dangerously radioactive substances.

"We have concluded that no form of creature dependent on lungs could develop or survive in such an atmosphere. Our anthropologists hypothesize that whatever listens to a 'Bing Crosby' must be a lungless form of life, perhaps a hideous permutation of the biped which, like some monstrous walking vulture, has adapted itself to living on atmospheric garbage.

"How eerie it is to think of these walking garbage breathers gulping draughts of noxious carbon and sulphur and listening night and day to their Bing Crosby's lamenting for 'A White Christmas.' It would not be surprising if they responded with great viciousness to any Venusian scientific expedition.

"The radioactive air samples suggest an experimental interest in nuclear physics. It is our best guess that the garbage breathers, desperate perhaps to relieve the misery of their frozen environment have sought to warm their world with atomic explosions.

"A minority believes, however, that these explosions result from warfare. Our radio data suggest an elementary tribal form of political life of almost animal bestiality, but few of us believe that such primitive tribal groupings could survive if they had the knowledge to package nuclear energy in weapons.

"In any case, the planet scarcely seems worth closer exploration. In view of the overwhelming evidence of its utter hostility to the higher forms of life, we suggest that no further expenditures be made to put a Venusian on earth and that, instead, we initiate a crash program to make the more exciting trip to Mars."

JINGLE BELLS
4. *THE SPREADING DECLINE*

What was so shocking about the toy racing car's triumph over the toy train was its swiftness. One winter the shops were full of electric trains sedately hauling freight up papier-mâché mountains; the next, they were full of racing cars whining round and round rubber roadbeds in the idiotic race to Nowhere.

The racing cars made their first mass appearance in 1962, and this year they are dominant. The old toy-train layouts are still up in most stores, but the managers complain that business is sickly and a depressing number of articles in the catalogue are suddenly no longer available.

Now, it is the racing-car layout that draws the crowds. Everybody who bought basic sets last year seems to be plunging on accessories this year. Business is booming in plastic guard railing, automatic lap counters, starting posts, track lights, refueling pits, plasticene hedges, grandstand boxes and tiny human crowds to put in them.

Soon there will probably be miniature plastic Monte Carlos for staging a tiny Grand Prix around the Christmas tree. Many dull sociological conclusions can be drawn. The most obvious is that children are responding naturally to an automotive world.

Most youngsters nowadays have had their first car accident before they ever set foot on a train. They grow up in cities that are being destroyed to accommodate cars and in homes where life moves to the tempo of the internal combustion engine. The train may be part of their folklore, but it is no longer the locomotive that starts long dreams of faraway places and adventure beyond the mountain.

The downfall of the toy train has occurred simultaneously with another apocalypse at the doll counter. There the sex kitten ("Barbie") has replaced the baby doll. What upheaval says more about the age?

The appeal of the baby doll was that she was a baby and utterly without precocity. In her expensive manifestation, she closed her eyes to sleep, said "ma-ma" when bent at the waist, and dampened her diaper if fed water from a nursing bottle. What the baby doll offered little girls was sound preparation for the realities of life beyond the "Barbie" stage.

"Barbie" is another dish. For complete happiness, she requires a $250 wardrobe and an adolescent steady ("Ken"). Should "Barbie" and "Ken" marry, the tedium must be relieved by "Midge," another sex kitten with whom "Barbie" can drink coffee mornings after "Ken" has gone off to work.

The ugly implications of "Barbie" are clear enough, but the racing-car layout seems a deceptively logical development of the old toy train. The cars go around on electrified rails, like the trains, and get nowhere. And yet everything is different.

The racer is a bomb on wheels. Its only purpose is to dash around the track faster than another toy racer. To break the mindless monotony of the speed, it emits a high-pitched insect whine, satisfying the modern craving for nerve abrasive, and occasionally roars in to the plasticene crowds in humdrum little mock disasters.

The toy train was a beautiful piece of engineering to be savored gently. Hours could be passed deciding whether the box car should be coupled between the gondola and the tank car for best aesthetic effect or whether the cattle car could be placed behind the refrigerator car without violating the principles of sound railroading.

You sent the whole rig up the grades barely moving, because that was the way real freights moved. You exulted in the glow of a headlight creeping through the tunnel, worried about switches, took pride in a skillful piece of coupling and fretted about making the whistle echo off the papier-mâché mountains with the proper tone of melancholy.

The train was a toy to teach a boy to dream. The racing car merely prepares him for the day when he will want to escape from "Barbie" and "Midge." Like the best of modern machinery, it puts dreaming in its proper place and makes life ever so much more practical.

What are we doing to these children?

JINGLE BELLS
5. THE MOST

In conformity with an old American year-end custom, everybody is busy this weekend picking the 10 most. The 10 most earth-shaking news events of 1962. The 10 most wonderful movies. The 10 most muscular moments in sport. The 10 most memorable books. The 10 most dazzling etceteras and the 10 most stunning and-so-forths.

The compilers of these lists are vulnerable to all manner of peril. Take the editor who has to pick the 10 most earth-shaking events. History is almost certain to make him look foolish; earth-shaking events have an ugly habit of happening unseen under the editor's nose while he is busy putting headlines on events that will be forgotten next year.

The electrocution of Bruno Richard Hauptmann, for example, was a natural editor's selection as one of the "most" events of 1936. Two years later when man first succeeded in splitting the uranium atom, however, the event made nobody's list of 10 most. It is a good short-odds bet that the earth-shaking events of 1962 haven't even been reported yet, and won't be for five or ten or twenty years.

The editors compiling the lists know history will laugh at them, but they are not in such an unenviable position as the men who have to pick the 10 best movies of the year. These fellows are always gambling against the strong likelihood that the last year did not produce 10 movies worth seeing, much less 10 that justify the adjective "best." Think of all the poor devils who still have to live with the memory that they picked "Ben Hur" as one of the 10 best of 1959.

This raises the question whether the 10 most lists, useful though they may be, do not impose unduly harsh demands on the people who have to compile them. What is the magic of the number 10? In a year that produces so few good movies that the reviewers must list "Ben Hur" to pad out their lists to 10, why should they be forced to pick 10 best? Why not let them stop at eight best, or three best?

Any reform of the old American year-end custom should also include a broadening of the categories. It is very nice to have the most earth-shaking news events, the most wonderful movies, the most muscular moments in sport, the most memorable books and the most dazzling etceteras, but these traditional categories tell us very little of our world's progress.

Why not, for example, pick the four least significant events of 1962? A possible list might look like this:

1. The patenting by James H. Jenkins of Athens, Ga., of a snake repellent compounded of ammonia, benzoyl chloride, and musk from mink, civet cat, weasel, badger and skunk.

2. The declaration by a British botanist that the forbidden fruit which Eve fed Adam in the Garden of Eden was not an apple, but an apricot, or possibly a quince.

3. The introduction by the Seeburg Corporation of a new "quiet" model juke box for "class" establishments that would not accept the old chrome-and-flashing-neon model.

4. The burglary of the quartermaster's store in Salisbury Prison, Southern Rhodesia, by thieves who broke into prison to get to the loot.

In these four items lies a tale of man's struggle and progress over the past year, yet each has the virtue of lacking depressing significance. They tell of man's continuing conquest of his hostile environment (snake repellent); of his struggle to understand his origins (apricots in Eden); of his maturing aesthetic sense (the sedate juke box), and one of his indomitable ingenuity (the break into prison).

There should also be a list of the one most humble confession of the year. It might consist of the confession of Assistant Fire Chief Frank Soper of Denver who, upon retiring this year, admitted that he had used the stairs instead of the firemen's pole for the past ten years. "I got so heavy I thought I might end up in the basement," he said.

Then, there might be a list of the five most unsurprising stories of 1962. For example, (1) movie queen, accepting Academy Award, weeps. (2) Yankees win pennant. (3) Broadway theater pronounced dead. (4) Disarmament talks collapse. (5) Says she admires God, mother, marriage; wins Miss America crown.

Someone will say that these lists are pointless, meaningless, silly. That could be. They may be almost as silly as the lists of 10 most earth-shaking events, 10 most wonderful movies, 10 most muscular moments in sport, 10 most memorable books, and the 10 most stunning and-so-forths.

JINGLE BELLS
6. *A SENSIBLE PROPOSAL*

When will American technology finally get around to producing an automatic Christmas tree dismantler?

Electric underwear was wonderful. The automatic pants elevator for assisting gentlemen in donning their trousers was ingenious. The turnpike toll gun enabling motorists to shoot coins into "exact change" baskets at highway toll booths was daring. But all could have waited on an innovation in the Christmas tree dismantling sector. A quick study of the Federal documents indicates that there has never been any progress made toward solving the Christmas tree dismantling problem.

This is strange, for while the problem is admittedly difficult, it is obviously easier to build a machine that will untrim a pine tree, package the trimmings for neat storage and flush the tree down the sink than it is to put a man on the moon and bring him back to Florida, which we are about to do.

The explanation may be that the Russians are not working on a Christmas tree dismantler. If they were, we would probably see a Government-sponsored crash program that would have Christmas tree dismantlers in every home by 1965.

The specifications for an automatic dismantler can be drawn up by almost anybody who has wrestled with the problem of getting a large, ornamented tree out of the living room. It should retail at about $150, which is the maximum that most heavily mortgaged householders are willing to pay to get out of doing the job themselves.

Considering that it would be used only once a year, it should be built to break down only every other year. The essential innards—gears, cogs, tubes, fuses, rheostats—should be designed of material guaranteed to disintegrate thirty-seven months after marketing. The machine would be sold on a thirty-six-month payment plan.

Ideally, the machine should be built so that its owner may preset it to go into action on a fixed date. When the Christmas tree is put up, for example, the machine might be set to dismantle it on Jan. 2. This would automatically relieve the household of those arguments, so common in early January, about when the tree should come down.

The children inevitably argue for keeping it up while mother argues for taking it down and father straddles the issue, dreading slashed hands from the dried pine needles but worried about the fire hazard. Presetting the automatic dismantler would eliminate all this. At its fixed hour, the machine would clomp into the living room and ruthlessly go to work.

What should the machine do? At a minimum, it should be capable of removing all glass ornaments with wire hangers intact and removing electric lights. It ought to box the ornaments in a neat pile and pack the lights without tangling the wires. It must also be capable of disposing of the tree, preferably by consuming it right in the living room and reducing it to sawdust packaged for the trash can.

It should also be built to use optional equipment, at a stiff additional price, of course. Undoubtedly, a big optional seller, like automatic transmission in the auto market, would be an icicle remover. There is a huge class of people in this country which believes it a sinful waste to throw out a tree without salvaging the icicles. These people would certainly feel moral compulsions to buy the icicle remover, even at a high price.

Then, there might be optional furniture-moving and rug-cleaning equipment designed to restore furniture to its pre-Christmas room positions and to remove those pine-gum oozings from the carpet.

For status-minded people who want to be able to boast about their dismantlers, there might be built-in music, ash trays and tissue-paper dispensers, colored lights that wink in shifting patterns as the work progresses, white sidewall icicle packagers. . . .

Well, now we must stop daydreaming and start thinking about getting those trees out of the living room. They get to be fire hazards, you know. Of course, it wouldn't hurt to let them stand just a day or two longer. Helps stretch the holiday. Of course, they do get to be fire hazards. . . .

PART 9

THE FAMILY CIRCLE

THE BIG BABY SCARE

For consistently bad news, the paper to read is *The Population Bulletin,* a deceptively arid-looking journal published by the nonprofit Population Reference Bureau. The bulletin's message, very simply, is that the human race is breeding itself to death.

This is a hackneyed idea perhaps, but P.B.'s ingenuity at embroidering it with attacks on the reader's self-esteem and with nightmare visions of a future crawling with people, people, people, keeps it lively reading. A typical P.B. trick is to catch the reader off guard with cheerfully terrifying little reminders that in a world as densely peopled as this one, he counts for little more than dirt.

"Happy birthday to you," the editors may say. Then, the twist of the knife: "You thought your birthday was special? Close to 9 million other people on this earth share it with you."

Usually, however, the bulletin is impassively proving that people on earth are going to be thicker than flies on a watermelon rind by the year 2000 and that there isn't much anyone can do about it. A recent issue, for example, turned a baleful light on Brazil, already overstrained with a population of 78 million and a growth rate of 3.6 per cent. At this rate, P.B. observes, the Brazilian population will hit 236 million by the year 2000.

P.B.'s forecasts of what is in store for China, India and Central America are the most devastating argument against romance among the underprivileged since Cotton Mather showed the Puritans the inside of hell. Moreover, people who think that a little breathing space can be preserved on earth by exporting the excess population in rockets are living in a fool's paradise, according to P.B.

A recent edition proved conclusively that 7,000 people would have to be blasted off the pads every hour of the year just to keep the present world population stationary. Estimates indicate that this would cost $3 million per emigrant or $500 billion per day. The feeling here is that Congress would find such a program prohibitively expensive, even if a congenial planet were found nearby to receive the colonists.

The bulletin never comes right out and says the population problem is hopeless, but faithful readers can draw no other conclusions. The editors limit themselves to assembling and projecting data, and let the reader's imagination do the rest.

Occasionally, they toy with him by springing a set of statistics which seem to offer hope. Invariably, these turn out to be full of hollow laughter. Not long ago, for example, P.B. reported that the United States could easily stabilize its own population within a few decades if each wife in the country would limit her family to 2.27 children.

Superficially, this seems a reasonable program, but it takes little imagination to see why it can never work. The flaw is that it is impossible in what the nuclear scientists call "the present state of the art" for any one family to produce 2.27 children. P.B. concedes the point but says the ideal figure can be attained as a national average.

All the wives must get together in all the subdivisions all over the country and subscribe to quotas so that total national reproduction levels off at 2.27 children per household. The Government has been trying for years to get farmers to operate on the same principle, and it just doesn't work.

It is as useless as asking all the husbands in the subdivision to get together and hold average gin consumption to 2.27 martinis per day. The man with a one-martini quota will rebel at a lower status level than his four-martini neighbor. The three-martini husband will resist on the ground that he needs that many just to do business at lunch. The two-martini man will lose his self-control and start cheating, especially if he is well heeled and can afford three or four. It is hopeless.

P.B., of course, knows it is hopeless. Ah, here is the latest edition now. "The situation is extremely grave," it says. "The period of grace during which effective action can be taken short of disaster can be counted in years—not in decades. The time of decision is at hand."

Anyone out in the subdivision for 2.27 martinis?

---

9 O'CLOCK AND ALL'S QUIET

September, 1962—The big news all over America this week is the outbreak of peace. After nearly three months of hostilities which took a fearful toll in human patience and broke many a mother's spirit, the kids are back in school.

Somewhere men are talking war, but the true sound of America this early September is the sweet stillness of the living room at 9 o'clock in the morning. In Havana the Russians may be taking over, but here in the United States the adults are back in power. Once again a mother can shut off the television without inviting massive retaliation. Once again she can dawdle over her coffee, untroubled by the fear that the heir hangs impaled on the back fence or lurks in the rhododendron armed with slingshot for the testy neighbor down the street.

In the silent morning air, it's again possible to hear a bird sing, to hear an acorn's fall. The yard is still. Here on last week's battlefield, still littered with broken wheels, shattered water pistols and unburied doll's arms, the bumblebee goes lazily about his business as though nothing really terrible had happened on this terrain.

One walks through the house half drugged with the peace. The wet-dog smell is gone from the boys' room. The living room sofa where they blackmailed you into that ghastly day at the amusement park—"What kind of a daddy would break his promise to take us to Happy Land?"—no longer seems a baited trap.

It is dark and restful in the upstairs hall where mother stood so terribly that night in August swinging the leather belt. What had it been about? Ah yes. Those big jars with the old seaweed that had been emptied out the upstairs window.

Already it is possible for the survivors to recall those tense weeks with a twinge of nostalgia. After all, the children will never be so young again. Remember vacation? The worst time was during that long ride through the Everglades with the rain coming down in sheets and all of them whining at once because they hadn't seen an alligator.

Of course, it had been a mistake to promise a quarter to the first one who spotted an alligator, but at the time it seemed like a good way to distract them from the fight over the seashells. After that there was nothing to do but buy them those little live alligators. Who would have expected them to put the alligators in the motel swimming pool?

Now, in the silence of the basement, the mind attempts to estimate the physical damages.

The garage pane broken with the tire iron. The knob removed from the bathroom door. Three palings torn out of the fence for battle lances. The roots of the cherry tree torn out during trench building.

Trousers galore ripped out in knee and seat. That hatchet gash in the garden hose. The slash in the billiard-table cloth. Green-and-purple chemical stain on the guest-room bedspread. The three rose bushes destroyed the day they found the scythe. It had seemed such a constructive idea to make them responsible for maintaining the yard. That was the week they moved the flower beds.

The household is scarred but it is now at peace. The schools have done their duty. The teachers are back on the job. Bless them all. Later, when the joy of peace has gone stale, we will all start complaining that the schools are not much good. Then we will appoint a parents' committee to tell the teachers how they should deal with our children.

The trouble, of course, is that the teachers are not doing their duty merely by taking the kids off our hands. They should also be educating them, and all the surveys show that they are not doing this adequately.

Later, when parental confidence returns, we will have our parents' committee tell them how to do a better job. Right now, let us not worry about it. Let us sit back and enjoy the peace. Compulsory universal education, you are wonderful.

HOMEWORK

October, 1963—The State Department is not the only party unhappy about Mme. Ngo Dinh Nhu's visit to the United States. For parents of pre-adolescent school children all over the country it means sorrow and trial.

Soon their youngsters will be coming home from school clutching those little newspapers which are supposed to keep the tots abreast of current events and mold informed citizens out of bubble-gum chewers. Mme. Nhu is the kind of subject that the publishers of these papers dote upon. Others are Gamal Abdel Nasser, Kwame Nkrumah and Joseph Mobutu.

"Kwame Nkrumah is visiting our country," their reports always begin, with disarming innocence. "He is from a faraway country called Ghana." With the next sentence, a Harvard professor of international affairs takes over and tells more than most diplomats want to know about Ghana's culture, history and politics.

This would be harmless enough if the child could roll the paper into spitballs and forget about it, but this is not permitted. Most teachers insist that the child test his grasp of the subject by taking the quiz at the back of the paper. "Who are the fellahin?" "What is the cost of the Aswan Dam?" "Discuss the anthropological history of the Ashanti."

Some parents take the attitude that this is a useless kind of knowledge for children who need all their strength for long division. These parents let the child muddle through the quiz as best he can after they have spent their energies browbeating him with arithmetic. These children, of course, are not going to make it into the better colleges, but their parents are the kind who tell you they would rather have a well-adjusted son on the relief rolls than a neurotic son on Wall Street.

Parents who want their children to move up in life either do the quiz themselves or spend hideous nights instructing their young in current events. Anybody who has tried to explain Congo politics to a ten-year-old boy knows what a toll this takes.

It is not hard to foresee what the Mme. Nhu visit is going to touch off. "Mme. Nhu is visiting our country. She is from a far-away country called Vietnam. . . ."

"All right, Rollo, I'll try to explain it once again. Bao Dai is not to be confused with Cao Dai. Bao Dai went to the Riviera and Cao Dai is an organization. All right, Rollo, wipe the bubble gum off your chin, and we'll try again. Who is Mme. Nhu?"

"Mme. Nhu is visiting our country. She is from a far-away country called . . . called. . . ."

"That's right. Say it."

"Ghana?"

"Come on, Rollo. You'll never get into Harvard if you don't pay attention. Mme. Nhu is from Vietnam. Remember?"

"That's right, Vietnam, and she's the sister of Souvanna Phouma . . ."

"No, she is not the sister of Souvanna Phouma. Souvanna Phouma is the half-brother of Souvanouvong. Mme. Nhu is the sister-in-law of Ngo Dinh Diem who became ruler of Vietnam after Ho Chi Minh won at Dienbienphu and Bao Dai went to the Riviera. Now, what's the difference between the Viet Minh, the Vietcong and the Neo Lao Hak Xat?"

"The Vietcong are the bad guys, right? Like Hitler?"

"Right."

"The Neo Lao Hak Xat is . . . is. . . ."

"Say it. You've got it. . . ."

"Is that the name of the yacht Mrs. Kennedy's staying on in Greece?"

"Look, Rollo. You want to go to Harvard, don't you? You know how hard it's going to be to get into Harvard when you're eighteen? You know that boys who don't get into Harvard won't have a chance in life because of the automation? Now let's start all over."

"Was it easier when you were a boy, daddy?"

"Well, when I was a boy, son, all you had to know was that this country was never going to get involved in any more foreign entanglements or pull England's chestnuts out of the fire again. Of course, it was easier to get into Harvard in those days. Now, who is Ngo Dinh Thuc . . . ?"

Mme. Nhu, why are you making it so hard for our boys to get into Harvard?

THE MINIATURE ADULTS

A great deal is being thought and written nowadays about the problems of the aged, but there is no realistic agreement about who these aged are.

It is not enough to define them as the people over sixty-five, or "our senior citizens," to use the unctuous euphemism. Everyone knows of the over-forty group, which is too young for Social Security but too old to be hired, and of the over-forty-five group inside industry, which is too young to be retired but too old to start up the management ladder.

But there are many aged who are even younger than these. There is the whole generation of parents between the ages of thirty and forty who have come home one afternoon, to discover their children practicing teen-age-ism.

Teen-age-ism. It is a terrible thing, not to be confused with adolescence. No one can help being an adolescent; it is a natural stage of man. Being a teen-ager, on the other hand, is the youngest profession, an artificial condition imposed upon youth by peculiar forces in the society.

These forces compel the poor adolescent to behave according to the precepts of teen-age-ism, a curious philosophy which holds that youth is a terrible thing to happen to the young. To help them through this miserable period, the theory goes, the old folks (in the thirty-to-forty bracket) must humor them in the conceit that they are really little underdeveloped adults.

This may be very nice for the adolescents (although it probably isn't), but it places an enormously unfair burden on the parents. If a twelve-year-old starts thinking of himself as adult, he is naturally going to start thinking of his parents as senescent ("square" is the word in common usage) and start treating them accordingly.

A mother of thirty-five years who finds herself being treated like an old woman, or a square, is bound to start feeling self-conscious about her age, no matter how frisky she may feel at the cocktail hour. Intimations of mortality will inevitably begin to intrude into her carefree moments.

"Drinking again, Mother!" the miniature adult may say, with only the slightest hint of censure, poisoning the moment and opening views onto a future of gray hair and failed liver.

"But you're too young for a Tony Curtis haircut!" the father may protest to his eleven-year-old boy. And the boy's "Oh, Dad! Get with it!" is a veiled threat to have the old gentleman committed to a rocking chair.

In these moments of despair, the old folks may occasionally remind the miniature adults that it hasn't been long since they learned to do the Jitterbug on the drugstore corner. A terrible mistake. Anyone old enough to remember Elvis Presley is ancient, and all before that is Egyptology.

The result on the parents is shocking. One day they are rocking contentedly along, thinking of themselves as "young marrieds," the stars of the American advertising drama; the next, they are simply "the folks" to a pack of cunning little adults, or, in really acute cases, "the old man" and "the old lady."

Can this premature aging be avoided? Probably not any longer in the United States nor in Western Europe. Teen-age-ism, which originated here, is traveling the earth like a plague. There is no reason to think that the children like it, but they have no way to escape it.

It is drilled into them by movies, television, disk jockeys, newspapers, magazines, authors, lecturers and merchandisers. All have combined to create the awful trial known as "teen-age" and to teach the wretched young how to survive it.

Aside from the strain on the children, the terrible part of all this is the way it lowers the threshold of old age into the thirties. Some heretics say that a false sense of youth can be preserved if parents will occasionally lay about them with a strap, but the prophets of teen-age-ism regard this as unwholesome and warn that the teen-agers may retaliate by going into an expensive neurosis. The bills for analysis usually age the old folks very rapidly indeed.

PLEASURING THE KIDDIES

Parents who want to get their daughters off on the proper foot in life will have to do some sharp financial thinking if the present trend in debutante parties continues.

News reports of Miss Cynthia Phipps's party on Long Island recently say that even the best-heeled families were impressed by the scale of entertainment—the four tents with silk-lined tops, the 12,000 flowers, the 25-piece orchestra, the hogsheads of champagnes, the salmon mousse, gallantine duck, lobster with truffles, smoked rainbow trout on a bed of aspic. This is a long step from beer and bongos.

The party of Miss Fernanda Wanamaker Wetherill earlier

in the season was in the same style. There, however, the youngsters incurred unanticipated bills by wrecking a nearby mansion. Everybody says this was to be expected because we have not done enough to make the children happy.

What will disturb many parents almost as much as the cost of getting a girl into society in style is the trend toward orgiastic endurance tests. Like movies and baseball games, the new party runs on the theory that longer is better. Right now the partying pauses at 2 A.M. for eggs and bacon, then swings into the dawn, usually until 7 A.M. The mayhem at Miss Wetherill's party occurred between breakfast and teatime next day.

If the trend continues, fathers next year may have to charter the *Queen Elizabeth* for a three-day cruise. Eventually, a girl will be unable to hold her head up in public unless her parents have rented her the Isle of Capri for a week.

Some parents will draw the line here for financial reasons, but even those who feel that nothing is too expensive for one of theirs will wonder whether something shouldn't be held back for those long, dreary years of post-adolescence. A girl who has served salmon mousse to 1,200 guests at the age of eighteen is not going to be happy offering cheese dip to her husband's boss at twenty-five.

Many women now in maturity believe that their own parents went wrong a generation ago with excessive permissiveness at the time of the high-school graduation prom. In those days, it will be recalled, most parents could not afford to hire a 25-piece orchestra for all-night dancing at the house. Instead, the graduates pooled funds and danced at the gym or the Knights of Columbus hall.

The question before every daughter's father was whether to allow his girl to stay out until breakfast, customarily eaten at a beanery after a few desultory hours of driving around town shouting "Whoopee!" and sipping beer from a bottle.

This may seem pale stuff now, but in its day it was just as heady as gallantine duck and mansion-wrecking. Girls who experienced it usually discovered a bleak adult wisdom. The magic moment, clasped and prolonged, turns into an all-night binge and ends by being a bore. Cinderella's fairy godmother knew what she was doing when she stopped the fun at midnight.

The trick is to send Prince Charming off to bed at a decent hour with his aspirations stirred. Instead, he is permitted to twist until dawn and, instead of deciding to live happily ever after, he yields to the impulse to break windows.

Dr. Benjamin Spock, the authority on child development, says that "young white people should envy the young Negroes who are in the forefront" of the racial demonstrations. "This is a time when so many young people are acting in a lost way, not knowing what life is about, or what they will do with their lives, and in this sense the young Negro is enviable, because he has discovered what his job is in this generation," he said.

Of course, many of us will still feel the urge to charter the *Queen Elizabeth* for celebrating our daughters. They deserve the best, and everybody knows what kind of people get involved in "causes." But would it be possible, Cunard, to have it turned into a pumpkin at midnight?

CALL THAT SIN?

President Johnson gave the wrong answer when a reporter asked him to comment on "the loosening" of young people's morals. "From my observation," he said, "there has been an improvement in morals since my day."

It is hard to conceive of a statement more likely to turn youth against him. One of the few compensations youth has for the curse of being young is the illusion that it is pioneering new outrages against the old folks' morality.

"Look Ma, I'm sinning!" has been the triumphant cry of youth since social order was proclaimed. The time-honored rebuke is "I don't know what this younger generation is coming to."

There are sound reasons for preserving this trite old dialogue, and it is the obligation of the older generation to carry it on. Most parents nowadays could give the children lessons in peccadillos, but they forbear.

They pretend to be genuinely impressed by the parlous state of youth's morality. In this way, they help make youth a little more bearable for the young. Youth is given the illusion that its rebellion against the old order is new and exciting, and that it is really lifting the old folks' eyebrows.

But what if the older generations follow President Johnson's lead and assure the young that the old-timers had them beaten hands-down at immorality?

This sort of thing can only compound the natural wretchedness of young age. In the first place, it is repugnant to children to have to dwell upon the human frailty of their parents. Secondly, the young are certain to go into depressions in which they feel cheated, bullied and inadequate.

It is bad enough for them to be told constantly that their generation doesn't produce sluggers like Babe Ruth, fighters like Joe Louis, heroes like Lindbergh and politicians like F.D.R., without having to face the charge that it is also bush-league in sin.

In the old style, as President Johnson must remember from his boyhood, parents were very good about understanding youth's needs. Immorality usually began with cigarettes under the bandstand at the Sunday school picnic and proceeded inexorably along a well-charted path.

There was staying out after bedtime to do the Shag. Hooking school to spend the day in the burlesque house. Expounding the pagan morality of Omar Khayyám to waitresses. Strong drink at the fraternity house. Asininities in automobiles.

At every step of the way, the older generation encouraged the delusion that such daring breaches of established morality had never before been seen. Fathers laid on with the belt. Conscientious mothers sobbed.

Occasionally they did a scene. "What do you mean coming in here at this time of night smelling of beer?" "Boy, you don't really believe that Omar Khayyám message about the bird being on the wing, do you?"

With the help of the older generation, youth was able to feel its oats. A certain percentage went to prison; a much larger percentage turned out no good, and some survived to maturity, in about the same proportions that have obtained since Solomon's time.

Recently the popular magazines have been doing good work in assuring youth that its moral standards are rotten. It is even reported that at many colleges, not excluding Harvard, boys and girls are seeing each other with the doors closed.

No matter what President Johnson says, we must all denounce such behavior as shocking. We must ask, Where would the country be today if boys and girls of earlier generations had met privately without chaperons? We must say, there has never been such immorality.

Remember that, youth of America. And remember to tell it to your own children when the next generation arrives.

TROUBLE IN THE FAMILY

Three disturbing reports on youth, marriage and family leisure produced recently suggest that the American family has plenty to worry about.

Companies on Madison Avenue will pay good money for disturbing reports on the American family, and the American family never seems to tire of telling interviewers what an alarming life it leads. From these reports, advertisers psychoanalyze the family and devise new methods for slithering into its psyche and delivering a sales talk.

For example, Young & Rubicam, the advertising firm, has recently turned market analysts loose on youth. Young &

Rubicam's analysts found youth in bad shape. Youth told them it was cautious and conservative and was more interested in security than in setting the world on fire.

The analysts diagnosed an alarming case of spiritual arteriosclerosis. Young & Rubicam's president thinks it may mean that soup salesmen will soon have to stop shouting, "New, new, new soup" and start saying, "Soup just like mother used to buy."

What is remarkable here is the assumption that youth is telling the truth about itself, or even knows what the truth is. In his essay, "American Youth Today," Reuel Denney deplores the questionnaire approach to the young as limited in value. "What makes the inquiry even more difficult," he writes, "is that what youth is and becomes is determined more by the small group of the creative young than by its majority members."

It may also be questionable whether youth is any more cautious and security-minded nowadays than it ever was. In the main, its chief goal in the 1930's seems to have been a living income and, in the two wars that followed, survival. If its aspirations now are better income and survival, why should we be alarmed?

But market research flourishes on a blind faith in trends. In the market researcher's world events are always trending. All is change. A market researcher who went back to the agency and said, "Look, youth is just as cautious, conservative and security-minded as it's always been," would be soon replaced by another market researcher able to satisfy the insatiable demand for trends.

The Center for Research in Marketing has been looking into American marriage, and, naturally, it has detected a trend. Travel advertising, it seems, is placing increasingly heavy strains on marital life. C.R.M. asked the American wife how she reacted to those dazzling "live now, suffer later" ads strewn about by luxury resort operators.

The American housewife said that they made her mouth water and filled her daydreams with thoughts of glorious "live now, suffer later" vacations away from "household cares." The more she dreamed, she said, the more she resented her husband's oafish dreams of a vacation escape from civilization, of letting his whiskers grow in the wilds.

What's new about this? Man and his woman have fought this one for centuries. If man has usually prevailed, it is because woman has usually understood that it costs twenty times as much to vacation at a luxury resort as it does to let whiskers grow in the wilds.

The research firm sees marriage increasingly menaced, however. And of course it has a solution: "Luxury resorts geared to hunting and outdoor life for the husbands and urban sophistication for the women." Bimini mated with the Yukon! One doesn't dare imagine the price of a week's stay. No, the only sensible conclusion, if the travel ads are really disturbing married life, is that the resort people should stop tormenting housewives and tone down their ads.

And finally, Elmo Roper Associates has been asking the American family how it uses its Sunday leisure. The family's reply, not surprisingly, was that church symbolized "the essential meaning of the day." And yet only half the adults said they went to church, while two-thirds take a drive and the same percentage pass the evening watching television.

Obviously, the American family has not been perfectly candid with Elmo Roper Associates about "the essential meaning of the day." Watching TV and operating an internal combustion engine clearly mean a great deal to the family.

The lesson of all the surveys is that the American family is in trouble. The trouble is that market surveyors won't leave it alone.

THE COOL

June, 1963—The class of 1963, which is saying goodby to youth on campuses across the country this week, is taller, heavier, richer, better insured and more fully motorized than its parent classes of the Depression and war years.

It may also be smarter, but the important distinction is not material or intellectual, but psychological. The world in which the class of 1963 spent its youth was not just the normal generation removed from the world of its parents' youth; it was a far country which children of the Roosevelt age had not expected before the twenty-fifth century.

Sociologists say that the premature advent of the twenty-fifth century has put a terrible strain on the class of 1963. (Another distinction, of course, is that the class of 1963's psyche has been explored, tested, pummeled and diagramed by sociologists and psychologists with a zeal that might have destroyed the frail classes of the Roosevelt age.)

The men who went ashore in Normandy nineteen years ago this week had grown up in a world where wars could still be "won." The class of 1963 was still in diapers then; it has no memory of such optimistic times. It knows that wars can be deterred at incredible expense, but it is considered socially awkward to dwell upon what might happen if war should actually occur.

The class of 1963 cannot remember, either, a time when there was no television.

It is a class that smiles readily at its elders, perhaps because it has the straightest teeth of any class in history. It had the good luck to grow up in the age of the orthodontist, and its parents have spent millions and millions to stuff it with beef and contain its buck teeth.

Professional muscle-builders keep insisting that it is a class of weaklings, and yet its athletes can run faster, jump higher, throw farther and swim easier than the champions of its parents' day. The extraordinary breadth of its beam is caused not only by overfeeding by Depression-haunted parents but also by the parents' provision of automobiles, which it learned to drive at about the same time it was learning to rock 'n' roll and just after it learned to smoke.

Although it is now adult and will soon be telling everybody how to get to the moon faster and what to do about the Communists, it has no emotional response to names like Babe Ruth, Benito Mussolini or Jean Harlow. It learned of Stalingrad and Hiroshima, not from the headlines but from history texts.

A few years ago, when it was in high school, the class of 1963 liked to be thought of as "cool." Its taste still runs to "cool" jazz. The parent generation never did think much of "coolness," having learned under Benny Goodman and Artie Shaw and Tommy Dorsey that good jazz had to be "hot."

The "coolness" has always annoyed the old folks who learned the distinction between "a cold fish" and "a hot number" back in the 1930's and keep muttering that the trouble with these kids nowadays is that they're a bunch of cold fish. The sociologists again tell us that there is something to this, that the class of 1963 wants security before adventure, that it has shifted youth's commitment from Jules Verne to the Prudential Insurance Company.

This makes dispiriting reading, but it should not be taken too seriously. Sociology concentrates on the mass of clods and, for this reason, is constantly announcing that the whole world is a bore. The class of 1963 will not go forth from the commencement oration in the spirit of the class of 1939. But considering the premature advent of the twenty-fifth century with which it must cope, it is really remarkable that it has a will to go forth at all.

PART 10

THE COMMUNICATIONS MIRACLE

THE INESCAPABLE PRESIDENT

WASHINGTON, *January, 1964*—President Johnson's compulsive need to telephone is becoming a national joke. It is too bad, but it is hardly surprising. There is an old tradition that any Presidential vice is to be indulged with a smile so long as it does not affront motherhood or the temperance belt.

The evils of a telephoning President may not be immediately obvious to most people, who doubtless think, in a rather hazy way, that it would be nice if the President should call them up at home some evening during dinner. Here in Washington, where the possibility of a Presidential call is more than conjectural, however, Mr. Johnson's phone habit is no laughing matter.

In the first place, it means that you must keep up with a lot of very dull news. If the President were to ring up, for example, and ask what you thought of his State of the Union message, you would feel uncomfortable replying, "Sorry, Mr. President, but I never get around to reading those State of the Union messages."

Matters become even stickier if you have read the State of the Union messages and didn't like it. After all, who are you to tell the President his speech was no good? Doesn't the President have enough to depress him as it is?

There is really no way to escape gracefully when the President phones. It is useless to say that you are out and cannot be reached. This is only a challenge to the White House communication network, which can reach anybody anywhere on earth or in orbit at the President's whim. The sad fact is that there is no escape from a President with a telephone in his hand.

Over the last twenty years we have all lost one of our most precious rights. This is the Right to Inaccessibility, or Freedom from Communication. The Bill of Rights does not specifically protect it, probably because the Founders assumed it such a self-evident right of free men that it would never be challenged.

They reckoned without the miracle of modern communications. The miracle's boast is that it can produce anybody anywhere to talk into telephone or microphone, address a cable key or peer into cameras. Of course, there are some continents left where it still can't quite be done, but these will shortly fall.

The worst thing about the miracle of modern communications is the Pavlovian pressure it places upon everyone to communicate whenever a bell rings. When the telephone rings, it must be answered, no matter who or what it interrupts.

If it is not answered there may be ugly questions to face later. How many men, visiting in Paris, have had the phone ring and heard their wives in America demand, "Where were you when I tried to telephone you at 3 o'clock this morning?"

The old human right to inaccessibility is being replaced by the compulsion to communicate, not necessarily because there is anything to be communicated but often simply to keep the communication machinery busy.

The time may be near when refusal to answer the phone is no longer a legitimate exercise of freedom from communication, but a punishable misdemeanor, like disturbing the peace. It is already hard for many people to remember a time when they were not constantly accessible.

A man just returned from a long stay in Africa and Asia, where the communications miracle is still at bay, reports that his whole view of life mellowed when he discovered that he could be reached only by mail and that "if you got a letter you didn't want to get, you just put it away and forgot about it."

Back here it is obvious that our technical ability to communicate has outstripped our ability to understand what we are communicating.

And so, while nobody would want to deny President Johnson whatever solace he gets from his telephone, he should realize when he calls up for advice that most of us have been too busy being communicated with to have any sensible idea of what has been going on in the world.

HI, OUT THERE

NEW YORK, *October, 1962*—"Hi, out there, sports fans. This is Bill Bellclapper talkin' to you from World Series shaving headquarters where everybody is still breathless from the thrills of the first two clashes of the great fall classic. There's no game today, but they'll be knockin' heads again tomorrow in Yankee Stadium, right here in the big town, so there are lots more thrills coming up.

"And now, to dope the series for you and predict what's going to happen next, my guest today is Augie Sykes, all-time diamond great for the St. Louis Browns and author of 'Baseball Is My Racket.' So settle back, fans, with an ice cold glass of razor blades while we talk to Augie. Hi, Augie."

"Hi, Bill. Hi, out there, sports fans."

"Augie, how does the Yankee pitching stack up to you on the strength of what we've seen so far?"

"Well, you've just got to like Whitey Ford, Bill, no matter what kind of day he's having. He's a great little competitor and a great money pitcher. When he's got his real good stuff, they just don't come any tougher than Whitey."

"He's a nifty little lefty, all right, Augie. Do you think he'll have his real good stuff here in the Stadium?"

"It's hard to tell, Bill. When you're out there on the mound tossing them down the pipe to really great competitors like Mays and Cepeda and Alou, you just can't let up. One thing I won't hesitate to say, Whitey'll be all heart out there on that mound."

"No doubt about that, Augie. There's something about playing in the Stadium that brings the heart out in every ballplayer."

"They know the ghosts are looking down on them, Bill. The Babe. The Iron Horse. The old Yankee Clipper himself sitting up there in the press box. Playing out there in the house that Ruth built. It gets a player right here, Bill."

"What do you think of Maris's performance so far, Augie?"

"Roger is a great competitor, Bill, he's one of the greats."

"How would you rate him in comparison with Mantle?"

"Well, you've got to say that Mantle is one of the great competitors of our time, Bill. Just being on the field, he lifts the whole team up. But you can't take anything away from Roger. He's one of the really great competitors."

"You've played the game yourself, Augie, and you know what it's like when the pressure's on. What do you think the boys from the senior circuit are feeling as they think about their first series appearance in the big town?"

"Well, Bill, playing for the Browns, I never had that kind of pressure to worry about, but I'd say they must be pretty tense. You've just got to be tense when you think about all those ghosts looking down on you up there in the Stadium. Of course, you've got to remember those Giants are pros, Bill. They showed against the Dodgers that they've got the heart and the hustle that make great competitors."

"How do you figure the Giants, Augie?"

"Bill, they're all great competitors and you've just got to say that the Yankees have their work cut out for them. This is a team that never gives up. I wouldn't hesitate to say that these are both great teams."

"You'd have to go a long way back to find two greater, Augie."

"Yes, and even if you go all the way back to the old Yankees when Rolfe was holding down the hot corner and

DiMag was roaming the pasture, or back to the old Gashouse Gang, I don't think you'd find two teams that had more will to win."

"In the light of all that, Augie, which team is going to come out of this flying the gonfalon of the 1962 World Champions?"

"Well, from everything we've seen out on the Coast, Bill, you've got to say that this thing is far from over. The game is never over until the last man is out, and that goes double when you've got a bunch of hustlers that want to win as much as these two teams want to win. I wouldn't hesitate to say that this series is going to be decided by what happens in the next few games."

"And that, sports fans, is the prediction of Augie Sykes. We'll be right back to see why Augie is calling it this way right after this shave by Casey Stengel."

COMMUNICATORS IN THE HEARTLAND

VINCENNES, Ind., *August, 1962*—Dr. Creswell Bates, celebrated American pulsetaker with headquarters at the National Press Club Bar in Washington, turned up here after a pulsetaking tour along the Ohio Valley. A conversation ensued.

Traveler: What a surprise to see you out here on the banks of the Wabash, Doctor. Back in Washington they say you haven't traveled beyond Chevy Chase since you called the 1948 election for Dewey after touring the country disguised as a hog feed salesman.

Bates: A vicious canard. Actually, I have traveled exhaustively for the last forty-eight hours taking pulses all through West Virginia, Kentucky and Indiana. It's wonderful to get out here in the American heartland and find out what the country is thinking about.

Traveler: It's marvelous how you do it, Doctor. I've been traveling the same territory myself, but nobody ever really opens up except filling-station attendants and waitresses. I can't honestly go back to Washington and report what the heartland thinks about the Common Market and Berlin and JFK on the basis of those interviews.

Bates: Or course not. You have to talk to the people—bankers, farmers and truck drivers.

Traveler: I tried to talk to a truck driver at a lunch counter in Salt Lick, Ky., about the Common Market. He looked as if he was about to punch me in the nose, so I dropped the subject. In Palmyra, Ind., I asked a farmer how he felt about JFK. "My politics is my business," he said. In Paoli, Ind., I asked a housewife if she was alarmed about the Berlin situation. "If you're another one of those encyclopedia salesmen, you're just wasting your time on me," she said.

Bates: Very good, very good indeed. It checks perfectly with my own findings in the heartland.

Traveler: How so?

Bates: The region is tense and, therefore, in an explosive mood. In this mood it would probably support strong measures in Berlin, but would also probably welcome a chance to strike at JFK in the forthcoming election.

Traveler: Isn't that a rather sweeping generalization? Personally, it just seems to me everybody is irritable because of the heat. After all, the temperature has been nearly 100 degrees for a week.

Bates: You'll never make a pulsetaker with that attitude. Have a little confidence in yourself, man. Don't be afraid of drawing conclusions. Keep your eye open for local phenomena, then interpret.

Traveler: Well, I noted a phenomenon in Shoals, Ind., where I stopped for lunch today. When you order a hamburger in Shoals, they put mayonnaise on it. There's a phenomenon. You interpret it.

Bates: Now you're mocking me. Listen, you leave Washington and strike out down the Ohio Valley to find what the country is thinking. You stop for gas in Kentucky. What happens!

Traveler: I say to the man, "Fill it up," and while he is cleaning the windshield, very casually, "What's the talk out here about how Kennedy's doing in Washington?" He says, "Oh, you don't hear people talk much about it around here. What's the talk about JFK in Washington?" You wind up giving him a ten-minute analysis of the Washington scene.

Bates: That is the classic example of how not to take a pulse. What you must do is back your man into the subject by first getting him to talk about local problems. Start by asking him what people in his community are worried about.

Traveler: I tried that outside of New Albany, Ind. "What are people around here upset about?" I asked a roadside fruit stand operator. "Hawks," he said. "Hawks?" "Yeah. Hawks has been after the chickens something awful this month." "You don't say? Well, what do you think of the way things are going in Washington?" "Seems to me they worry too much in Washington about what's going on over in Europe and don't do anything about the troubles right here in this country." "Is that so? Where do you think the Government is letting the country down?" "People around here think there's got to be something done about these hawks."

Bates: Has it ever occurred to you that you just may not be cut out to be a pulsetaker?

Traveler: Only too vividly these last few days. What can I say when they ask me back in Washington what the country is talking about? Shall I say that southern Indiana is worried about hawks?

Bates: Highly unprofessional. What you say if you want to sound like a real pulsetaker is this: Washington is losing touch with the country. Apathy contends with restlessness all along the Ohio Valley, and unless somebody in Washington re-establishes contact with the mood of the country there will be some surprised politicians when the ballots are counted this fall.

Traveler: That says absolutely nothing.

Bates: Precisely, my man. Precisely.

A MATTER OF SHOES

December, 1963—How much grayer life under capitalism would be without magazines like *Holiday*. At a time of year when most people are sitting around in clammy shoes watching the bills rise and listening for the tax collector's footfall, these magazines help us all to go on.

Here is the new *Holiday* with thirty full-color pictures of the good life in "velvet Europe" and text to match. "It was last winter that I glimpsed him on the farthest tip of the Cannes Yacht Club jetty, the gray of his flannels impeccably matched to that of his temples, his blazer glowing faintly with an ancient coat of arms, his figure enveloped by the Mediterranean sunset and the casino lights," the text begins.

The reader wiggles cold toes and yields to the vision of beautiful people doing beautiful winter things in velvet Europe. *Holiday,* which suffers from the Quaker honesty of its Philadelphia forebears, notes that velvet Europe is only for the very rich, but it is not above tormenting a nation of middle-class dreamers.

Here is the inevitable countess on a sleigh ride. (Are duchesses out of style? They never appear anymore in these velvet Europe layouts.) Here, the treasure-filled villa where one faces days "packed with charitable projects." Here, the sun-kissed habitués of the "champagne circuit" and the gloriously "unbuttoned gaiety" of life at Klosters.

A long immersion in this kind of fantasy is tonic for the spirit. It gets the mind off the inevitabilities of life and diverts it to the possibilities. In this exuberant society, is it not possible for even the cold-toed to reach velvet ground?

The answer, of course, is no. One of the sharpest class divisions in the society is the one between people and beautiful people.

The singular characteristic of beautiful people is their insulation from the natural laws that govern people. What, for example, makes it possible for them to winter in Jamaica, toboggan at St. Moritz and enjoy the gloriously unbuttoned gaiety of Klosters? The answer is winter-soluble children.

When people contemplate a winter vacation, they immediately run head-on into the question, "What are we going to do with the children?" They can arrange to fly now, pay later and ski now, pay later, but what will they do with the children?

The beautiful people never have this problem. Their children go into suspension with the first frost and stay that way until their parents come back to open the flower shows. It used to be thought that the beautiful people were all too young to have children, but this is not so.

The error was based on the observation that the beautiful people never age. In fact, they do get older but at a much slower rate than people. The reason they age so slowly is because they spend so much time vacationing, instead of sitting around in clammy shoes wondering if it's worth going on.

One of their greatest advantages is the durability of their capital goods. Shoes are an excellent case in point. When these people buy shoes, the shoes may last for fifteen or twenty years. They are fond of showing you their shoes and remarking that they wore them to King George VI's coronation.

When other people buy shoes, the shoes immediately start to deteriorate. The typical buyer of new shoes assumes that, having cleared this basic financial hurdle, he can now start saving for the velvet life at Gstaad. He instantly discovers, however, that his old overcoat is worn out and needs replacing. Then his roof starts leaking. Next his car breaks down. Soon his shoes have worn out again, and the treadmill starts another cycle.

The beautiful people are able to relax in Gstaad velvet because the shoes, overcoats, houses and cars which they buy are good for life. Having only negligible maintenance and repair bills, they have little to do except live beautifully.

It is comforting to know that there are such people. The knowledge gives us all reason to keep dreaming.

It is probably unhealthy to face the reality. The man with cold toes and a sense of impending tax collections needs for his own good and the country's to see himself idealized. He may be nothing but a rapid ager in obsolescent shoes with children who won't go away, but somebody has to keep him going so the beautiful people can have a velvet place to do beautiful things on.

THE LAST ROUNDUP

"Once again telegenic news invites you to join us for our annual year-end roundup of telegenic correspondents from around the world. We are rounding up the last of them now and are ready to bring you our portentous review of 1962 and to tell you what to look forward to in 1963. Shad Bunbun, our man home from Paris, would you start the ball rolling?"

"Of course, Charles. 1937 was a year of cruel decisions for Paris, a year in which Nazi power, massing behind the Rhine, and Communist agitation, massing in front of the Rhine. . . ."

"Uh—Shad, excuse me, but we are reviewing the year 1962. You seem to have a script reviewing the year 1937. Could you tell us a little about 1962 and something of what we might expect in 1963?"

"Of course, Charles. I think we can say without fear of saying anything that 1963 is going to be quite a year in Paris. Student riots, new styles for women, continuing wine consumption—these will all be factors to be reckoned with in 1963. Would you agree with that, from your vantage point in Berlin, Bucky Shores?"

"Uh—Shad. This is Charles again. Would you put that same question to Marv Stopes, our man home from Tokyo? We haven't quite rounded up Bucky yet."

"Am I really on camera now?"

"You really are, Marv Stopes."

"Boy. Do you realize this is the first time I've been on camera since last year's roundup?"

"Uh—Marv Stopes, would you agree with what Shad Bunbun says about the situation as seen from Paris?"

"Charles, there is only one question agitating Japan as 1962 ends. Japan wants to know why there's never any television news of Japan on American networks. I haven't been on the screen here since last December. It's this kind of treatment that has fed the fanning fires of Japanese anti-Americanism."

"Excuse me, Marv Stopes."

"Who are you?"

"I am Sandy Van Sandies, our man home from the White House in Washington, and I would like to know if the Japanese have forgiven us yet for Pearl Harbor."

"No, Sandy they have not and unless we scrap our nuclear weapons I see very little chance that they will forgive us during 1963."

"Uh—Sandy, this is Charles. Could you tell us what the upsurge of culture in Washington portends for 1963?"

"I think it's this simple Charles: Culture has replaced the homburg in Washington. This means that if you want to get the gravy these days you've got to have culture. I mean, go see the Mona Lisa, drink dry sherry, talk up Pablo Casals. That kind of thing. How has our new culture affected Latin American attitudes toward us in 1962, Sidney Henbane, our man home from Rio?"

"Sandy, no American who has had his best suit stripped right off him in 1962 by a howling mob of Latin Americans can be very optimistic because Washingtonians are going to see the Mona Lisa and drinking dry sherry. You have to remember that the Latin Americans still haven't forgiven us for getting the northern half of the hemisphere. What's more, I haven't forgiven the network's auditors for refusing to buy me a new suit."

"Uh—Sidney Henbane, would you excuse me? This is Charles. We have failed to round up Bucky Shores, our man home from Berlin, but we have just received a note from him which I should like to read. It says, 'The Germans will never forgive us for bombing their cities.' Would you care to comment on this, Carl Capper, our resident network brooder?"

"Charles, it just seems to me that it all means what it's always meant: Nobody likes us very much in 1962 and nobody is going to like us much in 1963. As usual, I think we can say the outlook is bleak.

PUNDITRY ON A DULL COLD DAY

WASHINGTON, *January, 1963*—The full meaning of the extraordinary ferocity of the winter weather, both here and in Europe, has still not been satisfactorily explained by the President, his spokesmen in Congress or usually reliable sources inside the super secret Central Intelligence Agency. Nor is it likely to be.

The reasons for this official reticence can only be surmised, but it is well known that meteorological warfare has secretly absorbed key members of our own Joint Chiefs of Staff as well as the powerful House Rules Committee since Hitler proposed turning off the Gulf Stream.

In the most hush-hush quarters here, no one will admit anything, despite the amazingly low temperature readings that have been registered all winter in capitals around the Northern Hemisphere. On the other hand, and most significantly, the White House has not denied speculation heard widely all over Georgetown that the dread weather bomb has finally been perfected.

The questions that must be answered are: Has science really succeeded at last in building the W-Bomb? If so, whose science? What becomes shatteringly obvious to the most astute observers of the world scene is this: If science has indeed succeeded in building the W-Bomb, the world balance of power has shifted dramatically, and this Government's immediate task must be to find out which country has achieved meteorological superiority.

No one can be sure, of course, but all indications suggest that the balance of power has, in fact, been changed significantly since sometime last autumn. The peculiar Soviet backdown in Cuba, for example, may well have been dictated by a third power secretly armed with the W-Bomb and ready to use it to prevent planetary incineration by obsolescent nuclear weapons.

If this is indeed the case, then both this Government and the Soviets have obviously been subject to meteorological blackmail for some time past. Small wonder the Administration has had no comment on the bitterness of the winter weather.

The more closely the facts are examined, the more ominous they seem. On every side the most extraordinary events have been taking place, disrupting a status quo that had given the world an uneasy stability since 1950. Even President Kennedy has spoken guardedly of "the winds of change."

He was referring, of course, to such extraordinary events as the ideological fight in the Communist world, the phenomenal economic boom in Western Europe, the Chinese assault on India and the trade which sent Luis Aparicio from the Chicago White Sox to the Baltimore Orioles. Obviously, something remarkable has unhinged the old world which influential members of the key Senate Foreign Relations Committee had come to know through extensive foreign travel at public expense.

Is the W-Bomb, then, a reality? Is meteorological warfare at last a horrible fact of our time? In the absence of any official guidance, we can only conclude that the possibility deserves agonized speculation. What we know for certain is this one ominous fact: The coldness of the present winter throughout the free world has been unparalleled, unexampled and unprecedented in the memory of veteran winter observers.

If it is true that the threat of meteorological retaliation is now being held over both Moscow and Washington—and who could read the season's weather news as anything but evidence of a massive demonstration of someone's ability to paralyze civilization?—it should not be hard for the voters to guess who is behind it. Need we look farther than Paris?

Americans, sensitive as they are to the historic emotional ties between this country and France, will find it hard to believe that General de Gaulle would choose to have the United States encased in ice in order to achieve grandeur for France. Preposterous as the charge may be, there are diners all over Georgetown who insist that the General's treatment of Britain proves him emotionally capable of freezing all the fruit in Florida if we try to face him eyeball-to-eyeball.

True friends of France, naturally, will hope that this speculation proves to be pure fantasy. Some Francophiles, in fact, are already saying that the unusual bitterness of the present winter is actually caused only by last year's nuclear bomb tests.

Regrettably, the White House will neither confirm nor deny this alarming speculation, but key super secret Congressmen have hinted that. . . .

ENGLENCH

Paris reports a movement afoot to drive English out of the French language. Its Tom Paine is Prof. René Etiemble of the Sorbonne, whose book, "Parlez-Vous Franglais?", calls upon Frenchmen to repel such corrupting Anglicisms as "snack-bar," "le knockout" and "dinky toys" before it is too late.

The English infiltration of French has been heavy since World War II, and the professor seems to feel that a France speaking "Franglais" is ripe for plucking by meretricious dollar imperialism. The dollar, warns M. Etiemble, is out "to kill our language."

Citizens of the English-speaking world should not interpret the attack on "Franglais" as a slur on their tongue. Instead we should seize the occasion to purge our own language of the Gallicisms that make us vulnerable to French cultural colonialism.

If France is threatened by "Franglais," the United States has been bled for years by "Englench," an evil language which mobilizes the nasalized "n," the *accent aigu* and the silent consonant to bully and demoralize the pure English speaker.

The purpose of "Englench" is to destroy the English speaker's psychological security by making him feel like a provincial. By destroying his defenses, it makes him an easy mark for those who are out to gull him.

When, for example, the English speaker sees a menu offering "hors d'oeuvres" or "canapes," he expects the meal to cost more than it is worth. Will he protest? He doesn't dare. Argument might require him to pronounce "hors d'oeuvres," thus making him the laughing stock of the restaurant. He pays up, feeling cheated, spineless, incompetent and wretched. He is a victim of "Englench."

If "Englench" were banned, the restaurant would have to use the English term for "hor d'oeuvres," which is "soggy sandwiches." The price of the meal would be realistic and the diner would rise from the table without needing his psychiatrist.

In dozens of mercantile situations, however, "Englench" undermines economic and mental security. The cowed English speaker pays through the nose when he sees "chapeaux" (overpriced hats); "peignoir" (robe); "negligee" (nightgown); "chemise" (dress for skinny women); "cinema" (flossy movie); "paté" (liverwurst); "chic" (expensive); "haute cuisine" (fancy cooking); or "potato du jour" (yesterday's potatoes).

What a hollow sensation in the purse it produces to enter a restaurant, to ask for a table and to be told, "See the maître d'." (Invariably pronounced "mayder dee." English: "headwaiter.") How expensive it is to wander into a lunchroom and find it is a "café," or worse, a "bistro." How costly to learn that the local "beauty shoppe" has become a "beauty salon."

"Englench" is also a weapon for the social destruction of English speakers. Who doesn't know the feeling of unworthiness that results from being trapped in a room full of people who say "passé" when they mean "over the hill"; "boudoir" when they mean "bedroom"; "rendezvous" when they mean "date"; "bête-noir" when they mean "monkey on my back"; "au courant" when they mean "hip"; or "bon vivant and raconteur" when they mean "Pierre Salinger"?

The interloper among these "chichi" (phony) "connoisseurs" (eggheads) of the "haut monde" (upper crust) feels "naive" (square), "gauche" (like a hick from the sticks), struggles to produce a "bon mot" (an elephant joke), commits a "gaffe" (compliments the hostess on her apartment's atmosphere instead of its "ambiance") and makes a "faux pas" (stirs coffee with his soup-du-jour spoon). Feeling humiliated, he hopes that no "recherché" (way-out) wit will give him the "coup de grâce" (knife him in the ego).

The time is ripe for a deal ("détente") with France. For a starter, we will take back our "snack-bar" and "dinky toys" if France will take back its "élan" (pizzaz) and pie "à la mode" (3 cents worth of ice cream for 15 cents).

YOUR METER IS DERANGED!

No one can dip into the Berlitz World Wide Phrase Book (Grosset & Dunlap, $2.95) without marveling at how thoroughly the American has immersed himself in the world over the last generation.

This pocket-size language guide for the modern American

tourist makes it easy to launch a romance or ask the way to the bookstore in sixteen languages, including Arabic, Swahili, Urdu, Indonesian and Chinese. When we reflect that not so long ago the typical American in Paris had nothing to say to the French after "Open the window" and "Do you speak French?" the implications of the World Wide Phrase Book are too overpowering to dwell upon.

Consider the exotic crisis for which it equips the modern American. Suppose that while tramping through Swahili country you are snake-bitten or mauled by a beast. In the old days, it might have been impossible to communicate your plight to the natives. Nowadays you proceed to the closest village, consult your phrase book and say, "M'wee-teh m'gah-n'gah." ("Call a doctor.") or, in severe cases, "Oe-nee-peh-leh-keh hohs-pee-tah-lee!" ("Take me to the hospital!")

In happier circumstances the book will facilitate asking the whereabouts of the bus to Kampala ("Wah-pee tehk-see in-ah-yoh-kwehn-dah kahm-pah-lah?") or finding a Swahili drugstore ("oo-nah-veh-zah-koo-nee-ahm-bee-ah doo-kah yah dah-wah?"). And yet, useful as it is, the phrase book suffers from the same fault that flaws so many works of this genre.

It puts questions on the tourist's tongue that will leave him recklessly exposed to answers he cannot understand. After he has asked in Swahili, "Where is the bus to Kampala?" he is going to be told where it is, probably at great length—in Swahili. Instead of explaining all conceivable Swahili answers, the phrase book merely supplies more Swahili questions to ask. "Where are you from?" "Have you been in America?" "What is your phone number?"

In this respect, the phrase book is not nearly so useful as the typical British work which always supplies a simple declarative phrase to supplement its questions. In the typical British book of French phrases, for example, the question for a cab driver—"How much is the fare?"—is invariably followed by the French for, "Your meter is deranged!"

This kind of response not only conceals the Englishman's inability to understand the cabbie's French, but also shows the Frenchman that the Englishman is not a man to be trifled with.

How much more satisfying if, after asking directions to the bus for Kampala and getting an incomprehensible answer, the tourist could instantly come back in Swahili with: "Take me there at once. I am on a mission of the utmost importance for the President of the United States."

The authors provide no such handy face-saving phrases. Consequently, the baffled tourist must take his choice of other Swahili phrases designed to help him save face by changing the subject. For example, "Send breakfast to room 702," "Check the oil," "I am from New York."

One theory of British history holds that the Empire's decline was directly attributable to its phrase-book writers. You cannot go around the world telling the natives their meters are deranged and get away with it forever, the argument goes.

The authors of the World Wide Phrase Book have perhaps benefitted from the British experience. Aside from "I have been robbed!" and "Get out!" they have studiously omitted foreign phrases with which the tourist can make himself obnoxious.

The American of the World Wide Phrase Book is not equipped to dispute, or even to defend himself. He is a gentle soul, confined by his phrase book to displaying "A picture of my wife," to ordering "five airmail stamps for the U.S.A.," to asking room service to send breakfast to room 702.

He will probably be a very bitter American when he gets home from his tour.

THE 21-INCH GRIDIRON

New Years Day—The football season goes on and on. The sound of the television set possesses the brain:

"Sturdepumpski flanked right, Tittle in the pocket. The

blitz is on! That's big Number 86, Andy Diogenes, crashing in there. Andy's a big one. Six feet eight inches tall, weighing 285 pounds. That's the kind of player you see every week in the National Football League. What about that blitz, Ray?"

"Right, Bill. That's the kind of blitz you see only on this network, and we're bringing it to you with all the color and excitement and tradition that have made the Souse Bowl the greatest of the New Year's Day classics."

"Excuse me, Ray, play is about to resume, but you made a little slip of the tongue there. Actually, this isn't the Souse Bowl, of course, and that wasn't Tittle in the pocket, as I said a moment ago. Wait a minute, there's a loose ball on the field. Somebody has it. Who is it? Yes, somebody's got the ball all right and gone in for a touchdown. Ray, find out what bowl this is and who's playing."

"Bill, that was a great recovery on that fumble and a great run for the touchdown with some of the greatest downfield pursuit I've ever seen. Of course, it all goes for nothing because the referee spotted an illegal mousetrap there in the line and called the play back, which nullifies the score. That's the kind of penalty that makes N.C.A.A. football the most thrilling sport on television, and only this network brings it to you."

"As you know, of course, fans, we've got our own spotters high up on the roof. You can see them up there with their headsets on, and we've just had word from one of them that this is the thrilling climax to the annual Tournament of the Geraniums, being played right here in the world-famous Window Pot. Wait a minute, there's a time out on the field."

"I tried shaving with the boop-boop blade and the boop blade, and if you don't like them we'll buy you boop-boop blades or boop blades, on condition you get into cowboy clothes and have a tall, satisfying glass of boop beer right now in Marlboro country."

"Play is resuming on the field here at the Southeast-Northwest Bowl with the Northwest Lumberjacks in possession deep in the shadows of their own tight ends. Most of these boys are playing their final college game here today and you can bet, Bill, that there's a lot of emotion down there in the shadows."

"Ray, you can feel the emotion of these boys. It's the kind of emotion you feel only on this network. Back to the game now."

"Right, Bill. Gumcrack up over the ball. Long count. Flanker guards roll left, splitback in motion to the right. Yurstitis in the screen, tackles shift to the shotgun, field judge and head linesman ready for the short flare, Simian on the handoff. He's going to pass! Way, way downfield! O'Bramovitz has it in the end zone! Touchdown! Listen to that crowd go wild!"

"I used to only get three or four shaves with the boop-boop blade but since I started drinking this beer, you wouldn't believe how many more boops I get out of each package."

"We're back on the field now, fans. That last touchdown has been called back and 25 yards have been stepped off against the Packers for having an illegal red-dog in motion. It's a tough break, Ray, but you've got to give these officials all the credit in the world."

"You sure do, Bill, these are the kind of officials you see only in the National Football League. They've turned back more touchdown drives than any other defensive team in the league."

"Excuse me, Bill, but I've just had word from our alert spotters that the national-champion Teton Twirlers, who are going to give us a spectacular half-time display of massed baton calisthenics are moving down onto the field. Those spotters do a wonderful job, Bill, and they deserve a lot of credit."

"Right, Ray. Now it's Staubach up over the screen, split wide, tight flanker flared left, loose end flanked tight, split flanker shifted into a tight flare, tight split flanked loose. . . ."

"It's just amazing how much easier shaving is since I switched from the boop-boop blade and the boop blade and started wearing these cowboy boots—"

"—tight flare split flanked, flanked split flared tight loose tight flanked right—"